ABOUT

Mickey Mayhew was born ... fashion crimes and rubbis... permanently excluded fro ... a little over twelve years old, but somehow went on to get five degrees – including one from the London School of Economics, a PhD, several published books, and his own semi-regular satirical column in the pages of the Whitechapel Society's regular magazine. He lives in Cheam.

Mickeypedia
The A to Z of an autistic savant

MICKEY MAYHEW

First published in 2020

ISBN – 9798655553323

A CIP catalogue record for this book is available from the
British Library

Typeset by Steve Forster
Cover designed by Liam Relph

For myself – I couldn't have done it without you.

Contents

Preamble

I sat down on the edge of the dock, legs akimbo, my toes almost touching the rocks below; just beyond them, in the dusk, the Mediterranean looked like nothing less than an almighty ink blot, placidly waiting for someone to come along and mop it all up. I took a moment to enjoy the view, before unfurling the drawing I'd brought with me, flattening it out with several quick passes of my palm. It depicted almost a simple stick figure, with just enough of myself – big brown eyes, white skin against disconcertingly dark hair – to prove that it really was a minor self-portrait. I then set about folding it up into the shape of a paper boat, this whilst someone came and sat themselves down nearby, a troubled look upon their face. They were maybe my age – forties – and seemingly quite fabulously French also; well, this was Marseille, after all. 'And what is this?' she asked, indicating the paper boat.

'Oh, this?' I held it up. 'It's me; or rather, it's emblematic of 'NT Me'.'

'Pardon?!'

I smiled. 'It's the me that might've been, if only my mind was wired the same way yours most likely is…' and then I almost warned her, almost divulged the fact that regarding current identity politics, 'NT' was actually the disparaging shortened term ('neurotypical') for those sans autism. But I didn't.

Anyway, she blinked. 'Pardon?!'

I shrugged at her, watching the sunset, oranges dribbling down into reds, lapping against the surface of the water. 'I'm letting him – 'NT Me' – go,' I said, eventually, 'I read it in a 'Batman' comic once, about putting all your bad memories into a paper boat and then just releasing it…' and I made a dismissive little gesture with my hand, fluttering my fingers out towards that spectacular sunset.

'…you're letting a little of yourself go?' – ah, now she understood.

I nodded, leaning forward and dropping the paper boat onto the water. It wobbled, righted itself and then began drifting slowly forward. 'I think,' I said, (much, much too melodramatically), 'that I've discovered my destiny, and so now I can let him go and just get on with it.'

She joined me then in peering at the paper boat's progress. 'But what did he want?' she asked, her hand lightly gripping my shoulder; really, we seemed rather like parents anxiously watching our child setting off for their first day at school.

'A career, really,' I said, 'specifically in the City – all suited and booted – but of course it never panned out how he'd planned.'

'No?'

'No. You see, when you're permanently excluded from school aged just twelve, well, people aren't exactly banging down your door to give you a chance, not when you've got a hole the size of an asteroid impact in your education…'

'But you…well, you have good work – a job – now?'

'Yes!'

'But not in the City?'

'No; no, I'm afraid not, much to his disappointment. And you see, that's why I'm having to let him go.'

'But, well, what do you do now then?!' she persisted.

'I'm an example.'

'Oh. Good or bad?'

I scratched the back of my head. 'Well,' I said, 'that's really not for me to decide...'

'A' is for...

…ableism.

Ableism is the prerogative – unconsciously exercised, more often than not – of the able-bodied and the neurotypical to treat those they consider beneath them – including the neurodiverse – with contempt, disdain, and so on and so forth, ad nauseum. 'Neurotypical' and 'neurodiverse' were coined by the autistic community in a spirit of vaguely flickering defiance at such treatment, to represent those without and those with autism, respectively. I've always thought that 'Neurodiverse' sounds vaguely exciting, like you're a member of the 'X-Men' or something, whereas 'neurotypical' seems just that little bit less flattering. I guess what I'm trying to question here is the wisdom of waging a verbal war on the mighty ranks of your oppressors.

For me ableism is all about intent, and as I said, often the malice that the word implies simply doesn't exist. I mean, buildings aren't deliberately built without wheelchair access; probably it simply didn't cross the minds of those who put forward the planning, although thankfully this sort of thing is changing. For what it's worth, I don't really think people mistreat autistic people simply out spite; they just have no real awareness of what it's like to have autism, and to process the world in a completely different way. This whole issue of autism awareness is slowly being addressed, but indignant 'finger-pointing' among various members of the autistic community flares up pretty frequently in this self-aware, politically correct age. Basically, these days it seems that some (autistic) people see offence in practically everything; one gets the impression these sorts of people wake up in the morning and wonder almost with a certain relish what might offend them on that particular day in question; being offended is the new national pastime, apparently.

Ableism first became an issue for me when my autism initially manifested, around the age of two or three. Now before I go on it's important to state that quite certainly autism isn't caused by vaccines, even though one of my earliest memories recalls a fumbling nurse stabbing a syringe into my upper arm whilst trying to distract me with a handful of soft toys. The distraction didn't work because I burst out crying and almost hocked up some phlegm to let fly at her; had my vocabulary been a little broader I might have accompanied this with a few choice expletives, like the possessed girl Regan in 'The Exorcist'. But at least for myself, the onset of my autism – perhaps indeed the decisive 'triggering' factor – might have had more to do with the unusual circumstances surrounding my birth rather than with the fact that I was vaccinated against this or that dreadful disease at a relatively tender age. I'll address the thorny issues of vaccines a little later on (under 'V', would you believe!). Now it's worth pausing here to point out that many autistic people – myself included – are blessed with a truly prodigious memory, but I for one can never quite lay claim to the feat of actually recalling in detail the facts of my own birth, certainly not in the way that one person whom I once met in a pub around the back of Carnaby Street could; 'What did it feel like?!' I asked, aghast.

'Like being too fat for the water chute but knowing that you'll reach the exit eventually,' he said, coolly sipping a white wine whilst observing my rapidly widening eyes.

You see, my mum gave birth to my sister Sue at home but several years later it was decided that she might actually be better off delivering me in hospital; she was almost forty (apparently the age of the mother can also be a factor in producing an autistic child). The labour wasn't all that long and nor was it particularly painful and so for a short while she was left entirely alone in the delivery room. Bored of waiting around – or so she told me – she gave one almighty push and out I shot. However, such was the shock of the sudden pain that she promptly passed out, leaving me mewling away for who knows how long, before someone returned and registered the fact that I'd made my worldly debut. So, whether or not this 'trauma' had some bearing on how I 'turned out' is hard to say. I'm not an expert on the various causes of neurodiversity but opposing this theory is the fact that the condition has proved to be almost rife in the next generation of my family, certainly on my maternal side. Therefore, my autism – and indeed that of several of my relatives – *might* instead have more to do with the matter of our maternal grandmother's close-knit Irish fishing village ancestry, rather than with vaccines or birthing traumas, although neither theory is really properly proven.

Several months after that 'incident' with the assumed vaccine and the overzealous nurse, I first met/imagined/longed-for the person I'll be referring to throughout this tale as 'NT Me'. Now, this manifestation of what to all intents and purposes was an imaginary best friend, coming in such close proximity to the vaccine, might be complete coincidence, or else it might not. To reiterate, I'll stick with what I said earlier and go with the fact that most likely it was complete coincidence, but I won't quite close off that avenue of possibility entirely. Anyway, it soon became clear to me that NT Me was quite clearly more of a wish fulfilment, an idealised version of myself, rather than being just your generic imaginary friend. NT Me was blond whereas I was dark, and he was buoyant whereas I was somewhat sullen and withdrawn; he might engage people in quick-witted and lively conversation, whereas I could only let rip on a very tight range of chosen topics, usually at that age 'Doctor Who', 'Star Wars', and little else besides. Apparently, this behaviour – the tight range of topics – wasn't yet reason enough to pathologise me, but my father certainly thought that by the time I became fixated on Spiderman that there was something very wrong indeed. NT Me was also quite happy to attend nursery school, whereas I screamed and wailed at being left behind in a strange building full of women with saccharine voices telling you to shove coloured plastic bricks into various different holes. I have a feeling I screamed so much at nursery school that I was soon sent home, probably on a permanent basis. This therefore counts as my first educational expulsion; there were to be many more along the way.

Having autism at this point – we're talking the early-to-mid 1970s here – wasn't considered particularly 'fashionable'; nowadays if you're not sniffing around somewhere on 'the spectrum' then you're about as naff as it gets. I was a trendsetter in this sense, at least. As for NT Me, well, as time went on it became clearer still that he was the neurotypical I'd most likely never get to be. We'd have a chequered history over the years, as a result of this dawning realisation.

My family lived in an end-of-terraced house in a suburban street in southeast London, in what I later discovered was perhaps one of the most right-wing boroughs in the country; the National Front was formed a few miles away, and the man who helped stage-manage Brexit – Nigel Farage – lived not far away as well. Besides this, our borough was the only place in the entire country that refused to take on board civil partnerships (or was it actual gay marriage?), finally being forced into doing so by the government. Out of all these, only the National Front really presented itself as a problem in my childhood. Had I been more socially clued-up, then undoubtedly a discerning awareness of its proximity might have served to give me a half-decent heads-up as to what I was in for over the next several years. I first happened upon them when the house next door to that of my best friend Simon Roberts was attacked – I was maybe seven or eight years at the time – and I can remember quite clearly being ushered past the sorry spectacle by my mum before I could ask her quite what the words 'Pakis out' actually meant.

My mum was a secretary – locally – and my dad was managing director of a shipping company, working out of an office in Kingsway, up in London. I had an older brother called Graham and also the aforementioned sister Sue, myself being the 'accident' that happened when they were ten or eleven years old respectively. Graham moved out to go to university when he was eighteen, although he came back for a bit after he graduated. I was quite close to him when I was young, sharing bunkbeds wherein I would lie there at night in my bunk, quizzing him on the meaning of life and why we were here and such-like; although I can't remember any of the answers, I do recall being reasonably satisfied with his general responses at the time. He was quite easy-going and humorous, although he had the rather disconcerting habit of dancing in front of the TV as 'Doctor Who' was starting, thinking that I would see the funny side of it; I didn't and would frequently swear at him in response, leading to a smack around the head from our mother and more hilarity on his part. Our sister Sue was more het-up; in fact, some people might have considered her highly-strung. On one occasion she became so obsessed the effect her teenage acne was having on her love-life that she covered her face with plasters to hide the offending spots, thinking somehow that this mass coverage made her look more aesthetically pleasing; as I said, I think we're all a little bit 'touched' with something unusual in this family.

As he grew older, my brother Graham became a Mod, dying his hair ginger and wearing a long black trench coat and big, lace-up boots, listening to 'The Boomtown Rats' whenever the mood – every five minutes – took him. This typical teenage behaviour culminated in the time he brought his friends round to slouch and sloth all over our bedroom, sleeping over and thus offering me the chance to wake up the next morning and find a pair of scuffed Doc Martens staring me in the face, courtesy of the Mod who'd dozed off down the far end of my bed; his name was Jason and he sang 'I don't like Mondays' at me repeatedly, until I drifted off again. Later, he explained to me why some Rizla rolling paper packets were green and some were red, and how such a decision might impact on his enjoyment of a particular cigarette on any given day. After that our mother put her foot down, and whenever the Mods visited, they were ushered out of the house at a far more respectable hour, and to leave their Doc Martens in the hallway when they arrived.

I don't have many memories of infant school, just a few snippets that seem to cover an entire two years or so. I certainly remember an aspect of my dyspraxia – poor co-ordination – surfacing when it became apparent that I could neither hold nor write with a pencil or pen in the proper manner. The teacher gripped my wrist tightly, the pencil/pen in my hand, and then she forced me to write in what she considered to be the correct manner, tightening her grip whenever the dyspraxia fought against the perceived alien influence. I recall allowing her at the time the petty victory of imagining she'd won me over, that she'd succeeded in twisting the tendons of my wrist into the correct formation, but to this day I still write and hold my pen in the most peculiar fashion; people occasionally remark on it and when they do it makes me smile. This difference – this dyspraxia – also manifested itself more noticeably in my gait, which many pointed out was rather a strange bouncy sort of a way of walking. This was a situation one doctor thought to solve – back in the day – by clamping my legs into a pair of callipers. These hideous clamps served merely to twist my legs – and my overall lower posture altogether – out of phase completely (irreparably, I might add), to the point where I pretty much can't walk in a straight line now without lurching about like a new-born gazelle. Playing kiss-chase in the playground at infant school, I clearly remember not being able to 'get' the girl because my walk – and therefore also my run – was so wonky; my would-be victim thought this quite hilarious.

I also remember the yellow tickets to be handed in for packed lunches and the blue tickets to be handed in for those kids who were having a hot school dinner, and that I always plumbed for the former because it gave me a measure of control over what I ate. Occasionally, my mum came and collected me for lunch, sticking me in one of those little red seats on the back of her bike and then cycling the five minutes or so back to the house, for a break of some forty minutes, before performing the journey in reverse. Those lunchtimes were peppered with viewings of 'Jamie and the Magic Torch', 'Chorlton and the Wheelies', 'Rainbow' and so on, all 70s kids TV classics; I loved Chorlton the happiness dragon, but I was so scared of his nemesis 'Fenella' the witch that I ended up having recurring nightmares about her, that she would snatch me away in the middle of the night when I crept downstairs to discover her lurking in our kitchen; I'm sure there's something vaguely Freudian in there somewhere.

Another fragmented memory involves cheekily pecking

my second-year infant schoolteacher Miss Duggan – with her 'Farah Fawcett' hairdo, so fashionable at the time – on the cheek before we left to go to the junior school. Junior school was only about twenty feet away, located in the adjacent, somewhat bigger building on the far side of the playground, this immediate vicinity meaning that you were basically stuck with the same class of kids for around six whole years, overall.

Out of all of these fragmented early memories, most pointedly of all I remember my mum walking me home across the top of the playground, when quite suddenly we heard a chant of '…Michael hasn't got one! Michael hasn't got one!!' being hollered from far down at the bottom end. When we looked, it seemed as though the entire school were taking part in this pint-sized and rather mysteriously motivated little lynch-mob. My mum rushed after them and they all rapidly dispersed, squealing and screaming as they went. To this day I'm not entirely sure if this event actually took place or whether or not I dreamt the whole thing – the whole 'ableist army' – up after all. There are many meanings one might deposit on this scene, some of them again perhaps a touch Freudian, and others maybe more mundane; of course, I've learnt doing five degrees that you can intellectualise almost anything and come up with crap, so who knows. One day I'll have to get around to asking my mother if she has any recollection of the event in question and thus whether or not it really was my first brush with the specter of ableism, showcased on this occasion in a more organised, intentional form.

I had one fairly firm best friend throughout my infant and junior school years, the aforementioned Simon Roberts, and besides him a couple of lesser satellites – Matthew Webb and a few others – orbiting my little sphere of autistic self-indulgence. Quite what the rest of the class had against me I can't quite fathom, apart from the obvious fact of my disability, back then undiagnosed but still painfully apparent in the gait and also in my strange, spontaneous turns of conversation. To my credit, I could devour a subject in seconds whereas my classmates might struggle with it for weeks, but by the same token they might in mere moments master a simple task which would leave me completely baffled. If you couldn't cope with lessons in those days you didn't have 'learning difficulties'; no, you were 'backward' or 'retarded', and that was that. No one in authority seemed to spot anything the matter with me, though; people were much more medically innocent back then, a bit less inclined to scrutinise every aspect of a child's behaviour the way parents do these days, which seems to be some sort of an autistic-style obsession all in itself. Probably I'm just jealous because I grew up in the dark ages of neurodiversity, before Dustin Hoffman's 'Rain Man' first opened up the autistic world to a wider audience. I do however remember back in infant school a class of kids who were kept apart from the others, and who were…different, for want of a better word; there might have been some disparaging comments about them from several of my classmates, but I can't quite remember. A few years later one of these 'different' kids turned up at one of the 'special' schools I eventually got sent to, but I don't think I ever mentioned recognising him from way back when. I do remember that when I said that I felt sorry for these kids, four of the biggest girls in my class – Anna Shepherd, Rhonda Main, Kelly Minto and Claire Shand – declared in unison that perhaps I was in that case better off joining these 'outcasts', picking me up and bodily transferring me to the nearest rubbish bin; it took two teachers, each holding onto one of my arms, to scoop me out again.

Although I'm fairly certain that I alone comprised the sole neurodiverse statistic in my class during these 'heady, carefree' school days, there was a boy called Neil Townsend who, by the second year of junior school, had developed such a foul temper that he would – on provocation – let loose with a volley of expletives the like of which none of us had ever heard before. Nowadays you might call this, in autistic 'lingo', a 'meltdown'. I remember one time bearing witness to this explosive rage and clinging to the skirt of our teacher Mrs Lovering in terror as the 'c' word and the 'f' word were flung at her with reckless abandon. It really was like watching a cut-scene from 'The Exorcist' played out before your very eyes. Mrs Lovering just laughed it all off though, in a 'jolly hockey sticks' sort of a way. Later on, Neil Townsend would try to impress me once by writing a story called 'Doctor Who and the fox' and presenting it to me like a kind of offering; I was, despite my general unpopularity, considered to be the class guru on all things 'Doctor Who'; 'Don't be stupid!' I snapped at him, rolling my eyes and then shoving the sheet of paper away, 'there's never been a 'Doctor Who' story called that!!'

That incident – and various others like it – stand out, but the day-to-day memories are pretty much lost in the unforgiving miasma of time. I still think I remember more things than most people do about their early childhoods, though; one of the benefits of being autistic is having a memory like a vice, which is wonderful when you want to conjure up something special, but rather woeful when you end up recalling a cacophony of crap alongside it.

*

As I said, it happens that my mother's side of the family was full of rather 'strange' individuals, including two male cousins who shared my name, and both of whom committed suicide when they were relatively young. Upon learning of this fact, I rather questioned the wisdom of my mother in clamouring to call me 'Michael' when my dad had wanted me called 'Clayton' (!) instead. This may explain why I later insisted on being called 'Nicky' instead (see 'E'), before eventually settling upon 'Mickey', which pretty much brings me up to the present day. I've never visited Tralee in Ireland to meet any of these maternal relatives, but they sound vaguely like the sorts of people you might expect to find inhabiting isolated, insular and rather inward-looking little villages scattered about on rain-sodden coastlines, families who can trace cases of eccentricity and mania back several generations. For what it's worth, 'eccentric' is still considered in some circles a polite, non-medical term for autism, although by the time I went to senior school in the mid-1980s the language normally employed was the more colourful epithet of 'f***ing spastic!' – we'll get to that sorrowful episode of my life soon enough, I'm afraid.

'B' is for…

…bullying.

My dad would often say to me, '…if you're being bullied, well, you've just got stand up for yourself!!'

In fact, these age-old words of wisdom were hammered home to me so many times that I think I took to repeating them over and over, rather like a parrot. Given that autistic people tend to take things very literally, it wasn't long before I was actually balling up my fist and swinging it out toward my latest assailant – Lee Woodcock – at which point it was practically 'Powie!!', like in the 60s 'Batman' TV show, with the sound-effect word emblazoned directly over the 'action'. Cue Lee Woodcock in tears and our teacher Mrs Tatlock in a furious temper, grabbing me by the wrist and slapping my hand over and over; 'You did what?!' she gasped, repeatedly; 'You did what. ?!'. As a result, I was actually expelled, after several days of being the bona fide bad boy of the school; faint derision at my obvious differences having briefly given way instead to a rather mocking awe; 'Got any more bright ideas?!' NT Me said, although the query was perhaps directed more towards my dad than to myself.

I was so despondent about this expulsion that I almost ran away and joined the circus – no wry sarcasm needed from you, the reader, regarding such an 'obvious' plot device, and no exaggeration required on my part either. You see, this was the late 1970s, and circuses with performing (i.e. terrorised) animals and even the odd exhibited 'unfortunate' were still the vague but rather unregulated norm; the tidal wave of political correctness and an increased awareness of animal welfare was still some several decades away. At roughly the time I got into trouble over belting Lee Woodcock, a big travelling circus came and settled itself in one of the parks near our house. I rode up there on my bike one evening and wandered about the place, hoping that someone might take notice of me. As soon as I'd been spotted by several of the 'acts', I set about regaling them with my ability to reel off great regurgitated reams of useless information at very high speed; 'We'll take you with us!' the bearded lady declared, hirsute hands gripping my shoulders (the facial fur, I later learnt, was actually a stick-on); 'We'll take you with us and I think that we'll call you 'The Remarkable Remembering Boy!!'

It was at roughly this juncture that I spotted my dad's yellow Ford Escort pulling up into the nearby car park, signifying the imminent demise of what might actually have been a potentially cinematic escapade. I slouched off towards him, pausing briefly as a light drizzle began to fall, turning and giving my newfound friends a solemn wave; 'Goodbye, Remembering Boy!' the 'Diminutive Doll-Lady' called after me, 'and don't you forget us!'

I was farmed out to a new junior school shortly after I was expelled from Raglan Road School, but I didn't take to the new place at all. The worst thing you can do to someone with autism, someone whose very existence is often based around the idea of sameness and routine, is to yank them out of their 'safe space' and plunge them into a wholly alien environment. Not that I really considered Raglan Road School much of a safe space, but at least it was familiar. The teachers there knew that I couldn't really cope with maths, but at my new school no such sympathies were apparent. On that basis, my dad wrote out a times-table for me to consult. However, when my new teacher in my nice new school discovered this innocuous sheet of paper, well, she tore it out of my hand and then yanked me up by the elbow; 'This is what a cheat looks like, boys and girls!' she declared, my arm still held aloft, my fingers suddenly limp and sweaty.

Eventually I was sent back to Raglan Road School, after one tumultuous week at the new place – I guess strings were pulled behind the scenes – so perhaps the whole incident might really be regarded as more of a suspension rather than as a downright expulsion; I think it was *meant* to be an expulsion, except that my mum took me back to Raglan Road School at the close of that first week at the new place and all but insisted they re-enroll me. On my return the following week, I found myself at the mercy of Mrs Tatlock, the teacher who'd rained down such scorn upon me in the wake of the original incident. Initially, she refused point blank even to talk to me, sitting me at the back of the room and telling the rest of the class not to speak to me either, nor to even look at me or acknowledge my presence in any way, shape or form. Perhaps she did this on account of all the bother caused behind the scenes, or maybe to uphold the feelings of Lee Woodcock; or perhaps she was just rather a spiteful woman, as it was patently clear to anyone who met me that I was mostly a gentle and unassuming soul, if on occasion a little self-obsessed and tactless.

I wasn't left long like some sort of a boy 'Hester Prynne', however, with a Scarlet Letter branded in the middle of my forehead, or wherever it was that 'Hester Prynne' was marked on account of being an adulteress.

No, the taboo of my temporary expulsion soon faded, helped perhaps by the fact that Mrs Tatlock left midway through the academic year and her unknowing replacement bore me no ill will whatsoever. Either way, the mocking awe with which my classmates had briefly regarded me gave way once more to the familiar sounds of faintly sneeringly derision.

Although I hadn't yet been diagnosed with autism, the kids at school had taught me that I was most definitely different, which meant that I was learning to expect short shrift even when out and about in the evenings or at weekends, and from adults who really ought to have known better, to boot. For instance, I was singled out by the owners of one of the local newsagents each time I went there for my copy of 'Doctor Who Weekly'. Basically, they would stand there with their arms folded, positively glaring at me from behind the counter; 'Do you think we should let him have it?' one would ask the other – they were an unpleasant married couple – before performing a mock bartering scenario, with one playing 'good cop' and the other playing 'bad cop', only they were deadly serious about the whole thing. If they didn't think that I deserved my copy of 'Doctor Who Weekly' then I would leave the shop empty-handed. I ended up doing a paper-round there several years later, although by then the place was in the more sympathetic hands of Mr Patel, for whom I would often take on the rounds of those boys too ill or too lazy to show up for duty. On these occasions I would often end up straining my back, humping around extra bags on a Sunday morning, back when the papers were stuffed full of free TV guides and the like. It was a strange, slightly eerie feeling to be cycling around on my yellow BMX so early of a morning, especially on the aforementioned Sunday, when no one else was up and I felt as though I had the whole world to myself; no one around to raise an eyebrow at my unusual gait, or to wonder why I might suddenly stop and fall mesmerised at the sight of a simple cloud formation overhead. For a while I delivered the local paper too, but that was an afternoon job, and the bundle of papers was so big that you had to do it on foot. As a rule, you were paid a pittance for delivering the local; on that basis, one of my school friends encouraged me to follow his example and dump his supply of papers down a dingy back alley, which I duly did; impressionable autism again. Several days later someone found the abandoned newspapers and reported me, and so I ended up losing my little afternoon job almost as soon as I'd gotten it.

By the time I reached the fourth year at Raglan Road School I was regularly organising gregarious – i.e. harmless gang fights in the playground, playful parties which pitted every boy in the class against the other under the pretence that we were rivals aliens seeking to establish a point from which to colonise the home counties. The girls disapproved, standing on the side-lines with their arms folded and their toes tapping on the mottled concrete. This newfound bravado on my part was perhaps a by-product of the expulsion incident from the previous year; I got quite good at organising gangs, utilising a quirky gift of the gab that the occasional autistic person can often wield with some considerable panache; despite the stereotypes, we aren't all gibbering wrecks huddled away in a corner and dreading the slightest salvo of conversation. Overall, I'd say that my social standing at Raglan Road School went through some pretty pointed peaks and troughs during these years; persona non grata one week and then flavour of the month the following. Apart from Simon Roberts, my relations with the other kids could change at a moment's notice, depending on how tolerant they were feeling on any given day; the same sometimes also went for the teachers, unfortunately. I wasn't invited to many birthday parties – invitations to social events tend not to flurry your way when you're autistic – and I only ever had one birthday party of my own, but that was my own choice. On the occasion in question, well, my presents were spread out all over the living room floor and the invited kids were all sat there playing with them…and I just freaked out at the sight; 'They're manhandling my gifts!!' I wailed. And so, my mum was forced to clear the lot of them from the house, with me standing alongside, arms folded, watching each classmate file slowly out the front door. If there were other parties going on then I wasn't privy to them, and my classmates were certainly very canny in keeping them quiet, if indeed that were the case.

There was only the briefest glimmer of sex in these otherwise innocent childhood days, namely when Simon Fishter went and unveiled a porno magazine that he'd procured from a draw in his parents' bedroom. Several of us pored over it in the dank, stony latrines on the far side of the playground; I took a quick glance over the shuddering shoulders of my classmates, my stomach lurching at the merest glimpse of all those soggy, entangled limbs, and then I hurriedly left them to it. Besides this, there was also a textbook in the school library with a graphic, full-frontal picture of a woman giving birth; I remember staring at it as though mesmerised, until the assistant librarian snatched it away, telling me in no uncertain terms that I '…shouldn't be wasting my time looking at pictures like that!'. I shrugged and wandered away, in search of something else that might perform an innocent, mesmeric spell upon me.

As I've said, my maths skills were certainly lacking at this point in my life – more horrors lay in store where that particular subject was concerned – but my grasp of prose was already, I think, pretty masterful. Often my teachers would flourish praise on me in their footnotes, sometimes embarrassing me by reading my efforts out to the entire class; trying to make me stand up and recite them myself usually met with scant success on their part. Mostly, the stories I wrote were made up of a condensed version of the previous weekend's episode of 'Doctor Who', but they seemed to go down well enough, nevertheless. You were awarded 'house points' if you put in good work and I won the most 'house points' for my stories, but little else besides; I certainly wasn't going to win any for addition or subtraction. My acting skills weren't much sought after for the various school plays either, but somehow my teachers always instinctively knew that I'd do rather well if given the role of narrator, which I went on to perform several times. Where the 'house points' were concerned, well, there were four 'houses' in the school, named after four famous climbers or explorers; I was in 'Hilary' house, but I never became fascinated with any of these venerable figures, however much their exploits were paraded before us during assemblies; some subjects catch and some don't, I guess.

We used to celebrate 'harvest festival' every year, and fourth-year pupils were given the privilege of being assigned a lonely old person in the area upon whom they would call, complete with a hamper filled with harvest goodies. Naturally, my assigned old person turned out to be the only one – for whatever reason – who wasn't around to receive his hamper, and so the headteacher – Mr Purkiss – decided to drive me around to said old person's house so that I wouldn't miss out on at least meeting them and perhaps handing over my hamper belatedly. I duly climbed into the battered old powder blue van that we kids had christened 'The Purkeymobile', and off Mr Purkiss and I juddered. My assigned old person – I think his name was Mr Russell – *still* wasn't there, this despite several large jabs on the doorbell from Mr Purkiss. I can't remember what we did with the hamper in the end; maybe we just left it on the doorstep. Several days later I went around to Mr Russell's on my own and I rang the doorbell, and this time someone called out, 'Who is it?' and so I said that it was Michael Mayhew from Raglan Road School and that I'd come to see if Mr Russell had enjoyed his 'harvest festival' hamper. There was no reply, but then a shadow loomed against the pane of frosted glass and five fingertips duly appeared, pressed up against it. 'Thank you very much, Michael,' he said.

'Well I'm actually here!' I said, arms wide, clad in my favourite blue and white rollneck. But still the door didn't open; 'Won't you open the door?!' I persisted, standing on tiptoe and peering through the pane of frosted glass, just catching a glimpse of a shadowy figure receding down the hall. 'I want to meet you, Mr Russell!' I called out, but he was already gone. I turned around and slid down with my back to the door, arms folded, quite utterly dispirited. I think I sat there for maybe an hour or more, until it began to get dark, before I got up, dusted myself down, and then hurried on home.

Towards the end of the fourth year at Raglan Road School – there was none of this pseudo-American 'Year 10' or 'Year 11' back in the 1980s – several teachers from the nearby senior schools came to see the pupils, trying to woo us with their various prospectuses. I was adamant even then that I wanted to be a writer and I think this dedication to my craft sufficiently impressed the visiting Mr Wheeler, from Ravensbourne Boys School; impressed him to the point where I was offered a place pretty much on the spot. This wasn't the school that my brother Graham had attended, which boasted some tenuous connection to David Bowie; having never been a Bowie fan, I never felt any sort of misplaced kudos from having failed to attend there. It was actually around this time that my 'problems' were becoming slightly more apparent at home, allowing Graham to begin gently instigating a discreet distance between the two of us, a gulf which has only really widened over the subsequent decades.

Anyway, despite being picked for the senior school of my choice, I was nevertheless quietly concerned about the move from junior – i.e. 'kiddie' – school to senior – i.e. teen/grownup – school. In fact, I'm ashamed to say that I actually cried myself to sleep several times at the prospect of the forthcoming academic shift. Now, this was most likely just your classic case of the average autistic reluctance in giving up a routine, even when another, equally regular routine looms large on the horizon. Perhaps also I simply just didn't want to grow up; I've noticed over the years that both myself and various other autistics seem rather anchored to a vaguely childlike outlook on the world, and for me the advent of senior school was surely a threat to that idyllic state of mind. And maybe I saw the incursion of senior school as a threat to the elaborate fantasy worlds I'd already concocted by the age of 11 or so; I didn't even know what homework was until I went to senior school, and when I found out, well, I resented the infringement on my leisure time bitterly. I think maybe I'd also seen too much 'Grange Hill', with 'Zammo' getting addicted to cocaine and 'Ro-land' getting run over as a way of escaping fat-shaming bullies. As it turned out, however, my fears were somewhat justified, with the mainly rather minor mishaps of my junior school years literally as nothing to the dramas and upheavals – and the incessant bullying – that I would encounter once senior school actually started…

'C' is for...

…captivity.

Well, on the surface this one is pretty straightforward. Whilst I wasn't a captive in the literal sense, there were occasions when I began senior school where it pretty much felt like it; oh, how Mr Wheeler must have wished that I'd gone elsewhere – to the Bowie school attended by my brother, perhaps – but I didn't. The school that I was allocated – Ravensbourne Boys School (as it was then) – turned out to be a wretched prison – almost literally – teeming with bigoted boys who did their best to make my life unbearable, basically because I was disabled. In response to this near-constant onslaught of vitriol I made it my mission to get out of there as fast as I possibly could; naturally this didn't go down too well with the various teachers, hence the term 'captivity'. I've lost count of the amount of times they actually locked me in a classroom in order to curtail my various escape attempts. Coming at all this from a vaguely pseudointellectual slant, you might also view this particular period as an example of a wider, more theoretical example of the way I was locked not only into a classroom, but also into an ableist society's expectations of me, this alongside the fact that I was also locked into a body that didn't always do what one wanted it to. Or not.

To make matters worse, the subjects on offer at senior school didn't suit me in the least; you can't force a curriculum on someone with autism, although realistically one can't really expect a totally bespoke education either. I had no interest in woodwork and I wasn't prepared to do 'games' either, certainly not after seeing one of the boys on 'Grange Hill' drown during a routine swimming trip. You might think that this aversion was also due to a natural disinclination to partake in physical activity, but I was actually one of the best runners in junior school. No, the trouble was that in senior school they took their sports so much more seriously that I found this po-faced intent almost laughable. Well, there was that and also the aforementioned 'Grange Hill' episode; this and the fact that Mark Tuffin threatened to push me over in the showers and then say that it was an accident; those tiled floors are very slippery when your feet are all lathered up with that cheap, nasty school soap. I was terrified of James Finch too, fearful that his spiteful threats and innuendoes would translate into something more physical, with the others perhaps egging him on in their football post-match fervor; it almost made me nostalgic for the days at Raglan Road when Rhonda Main and the others would simply settle for calling me 'fleabag', over and over and over, ad nauseum. I think I did about two 'games' lessons in all at Ravensbourne Boys School before I was relegated to that locked classroom, without benefit of books or paper, pencils or other helpful stimuli; it was punishment, you see, punishment for being so 'belligerent'. And so, for an hour or two each week I just sat there with my chin on my fist, gazing out of the window. I didn't know it at the time, but this would be a subtle practice for the years of enforced isolation to come.

Eventually I wound up sneaking out the school gates a

number of times, or else riding out of them on my yellow BMX in full view of my gobsmacked classmates; I loved that bike, really, I did. I ended up having to conjure increasingly ingenious ways of escaping rather than relying simply on the bare-faced brazen route, bike or no bike; tossing notes out the window to anyone who would pick them up was a favourite – we were situated on a busy road – and it certainly appealed to my burgeoning sense of the dramatic. I was of course also childishly naïve where the consequences of these notes were concerned, on one occasion almost plucked from an alley behind the school by a sinister, shabby man who'd first beckoned at me from down the far end of said alley with a sultry wave of his hand; after making good my escape I decided to sit it out in my solitary classroom confinement after all.

For a while.

The 'games' teacher Mr Atkins actually caught me flinging one of my escape notes out the window, marching me outside to pick them all up literally by the scruff of the collar; a light drizzle during the opening salvo of his admonishments had become – by the time we got outside – a veritable monsoon. This didn't stop his scolding, however, with special vehemence reserved for my reluctance to participate in his 'games' lessons. He then grabbed me by the wrist and tried to drag me in the general direction of the gym, upon which I began yelling for help to anyone in particular who happened to be driving by on the main road at the time. The more I hollered out, the harder Mr Atkins squeezed, until my trapped hand had turned a rather fetching shade of blistered red. I said to him, 'There'll be just that one nice person driving past who'll hop out of his car and save me,' only no one did hop out of their car and save me, in the end; perhaps it was raining just a little bit too hard on that particular day.

I think I ran away from Ravensbourne Boys School

some twenty or thirty times in total; it became a skill, something to be honed and refined, and certainly something that required a considerable amount of the aforementioned bare-faced cheek or 'bottle' to pull off. On one occasion I even went out in disguise, stealing a 1950s period 'costume' from the trunk kept for the storing of various outfits used in drama class; over the years I've become inordinately proud of that particular escape.

My parents meanwhile soon became wise to the fact that all was not well and adjusted their behaviour accordingly; the house was invariably locked when I got home, and I didn't then have a key. This meant I either sat in the garden until my mum came back from work or else I had to try and climb in through the kitchen window, if she'd forgotten to close it, that is. On a couple of rather risqué occasions I took the train to London instead, 'doctoring' my school uniform to make it look like I was a prefect. As a result, I was never really bothered by the police even though I was quite clearly a kid, and also – in my humble opinion – cute enough to be considered a paedo's delight. In fact, this 'comely' appearance led to me being propositioned on one occasion by a dour young man who approached me as I sat reading comic books on the wall of the fountain surrounding the Centre Point building. He asked me about my comics books and then followed up rather bluntly by enquiring if I'd like to receive a blowjob. I had no idea what he meant; to me it sounded like he wanted me to take receipt of some drugs or something, the word 'job' to an autistic person being taken rather literally. I made my excuses and then I went to ask one of the punky people who worked in the Forbidden Planet comic shop on Denmark Street exactly what he might have meant. The girl behind the counter – Amanda – peered at me through the veil of her Goth eyelashes and then told me politely that he was a dirty old man and that I ought to steer well clear; 'But he was young!' I replied, in protest, 'and he looked well washed!!'

*

Back at Ravensbourne Boys School, it was rapidly becoming clear to my teachers that I didn't have a logical mind, not in the least. This meant that maths – anything beyond your basic adding and subtraction – was almost beyond me; when I failed to make progress, the maths teacher Mr Clarke took to whacking me around the back of the head with his bare hand, hard enough that I actually saw stars. Mark Tuffin then declared that I was so stupid that I ought to be stabbed, skewering me through the hand with a pencil during the day's subsequent woodwork lesson; I had to go to hospital to have a stitch after the lead tip was removed. The same Mark Tuffin also jumped me from behind – what a hero – and left me sprawled in the snow whilst I was walking to my BMX, himself fleeing while I was still clambering to my feet, torn uniform and all. And he was also one of the ringleaders who eventually decided to bring his peculiarly toxic brand of bullying to my very doorstep, firstly by throwing stones at the window of our house and then – along with nine or ten of our classmates – setting fireworks off on our front path. Several of these classmates – a pair of particularly unpleasant Turkish brothers, to be precise – also took the time to send me a series of Christmas cards, inside of which they told me in clearest blue biro that they wished that I would die '…asap'; the feeling was mutual, but I felt my money was better spent on 'Star Wars' toys than on a responding packet of Woolworth's finest seasonal missives.

Anyway.

Eventually, Mr Clarke the maths teacher struck me about the back of the head one too many times and I got up and just walked right out of the class. The following morning one of the Turkish brothers confronted me within eyesight of our regular teacher, Miss Moss, and punched me in the stomach; she then pretended that she hadn't seen anything, whilst the rest of the class looked gloatingly on. I responded by kicking her cheap handbag clear across the room in a brief but brutal fit of utter petulance; 'I bet you saw that, though, didn't you?!' I scoffed, watching with a certain amount of amused disdain as she went scampering forth on hands and knees to retrieve her various makeup products.

On that basis I ended up in the office of the deputy head, Mr Lee, nervously awaiting a sound verbal thrashing. Right on cue he launched into his righteous tirade, just as I happened to fall under the mesmeric influence of the tick-tocking antique clock on the wall behind his head, a move he misconstrued as a blatant case of the bores, which perhaps indeed it was; after all, I'd heard it all before, about how very 'bad' I was and how very 'good' the other boys were. However, as a result of this perceived insolence he went and expelled me on the spot; 'Get out!!' he yelled, pointing a finger at the door, 'just get out!!' And so I did. If only I'd realised earlier that simply by making myself a wholly unwholesome prospect that the school would simply get rid of me, what hours, weeks and months of torment I might have spared myself! I think I did 'wheelies' on my beloved yellow BMX all the way back home.

After that edifying episode I spent several months under virtual house arrest; my parents were so fearful of the social slur of another expulsion that I was kept under the most rigorous conditions. Amongst the rules was the dictate that I wasn't allowed to go near the windows from 9am until around 4pm (school hours, roughly), nor was I to take any phone calls, and nor was I to engage in any activity remotely unscholarly; the comic books and various 'Doctor Who' paperbacks were packed away until well 'after school'. Many were the days that I simply sat by the back door – the parents were at work, of course – and fed the birds who congregated in the back garden. On these occasions I liked to imagine myself breaking out into a pre-pubescent refrain of 'Somewhere over the rainbow', before heading back inside to spend time contemplating the cut and colour of the living room wallpaper. Whole months passed that way, watching first one season and then another drifting by outside the windows; people got used to the sight of my sorry face at the window as they passed the house, my chin in my hands, watching the world go by from beneath the gap in the net curtains. Sometimes I still get a sense of that sort of displacement now, when I find myself feeling particularly socially isolated, peering in on the 'ordinary' lives of the neurotypicals with whom I occasionally come into contact.

During this rather tumultuous time, we – i.e. the parents and my siblings – were sent as a family unit to attend sessions at the famous Maudsley psychiatric hospital in Denmark Hill; it was one of the few times I can remember my brother and sister actually making an effort for my benefit, although I have a feeling they both found the whole endeavour deeply embarrassing. Every Wednesday evening, we would all sit together in a bland, featureless room with a big two-way glass mirror directly opposite, with a bunch of people positioned behind it, observing us and basically finding me rather fascinating; or tedious – it was hard to tell. A female doctor with an exotic name that I can't recall chaired the sessions and spent her entire time probing me as to why I didn't like school, why I was so dense in certain subjects and basically why it was that I refused to toe the line. When my school attendance sporadically improved, she would shower me with praise, but during my frequent breakouts she would sit there with her arms folded and tapping her pen on her clipboard, one of her well-plucked eyebrows arched at a rather disapproving angle. Nothing ever came of these sessions, I hasten to add; there was no great revelatory diagnosis that I was ever made aware of – this was the early 80s after all, before autism really 'caught on' – and so Ravensbourne Boys School therefore concluded that I was the problem and not they. In fact, they went to great pains to come up with an explanatory diagnosis of their own, namely that I was a 'quietly disruptive' influence on their otherwise orderly classrooms. This, I guess, enabled them to feel justified in their treatment of me, concluding with the inevitable expulsion. However, as far as I was concerned, this dodgy diagnosis sounded a bit like calling someone 'violently gentle', or 'salaciously chaste', but given the school's previous conduct I basically ended up carrying it around like a badge of honour. Perhaps if the doctors at the Maudsley had done a little digging – and perhaps if my parents had been more forthcoming with their family histories – then maybe someone would have discovered that 'bizarre' individuals were not an unknown quantity, certainly on my mother's Irish side. As I've previously mentioned, I share the same forename as two unfortunately suicidal cousins from that particular branch of the family; there must be a joke in there somewhere, although I can't quite suss it out. I do however find myself wondering why there isn't more research done into those sometimes insular Irish fishing communities from which my maternal grandmother hailed; the aforementioned suicides, several autistic people in my generation, and some rather odd behaviour even in those considered 'normal' all point to something being a little awry somewhere along the line. I also recently discovered that my Uncle Dennis – my dad's brother – was a religious preacher who frequently harangued people outside the local cinema, warning them of eternal damnation if they persevered in seeing the various movies on offer. When you look at it like that, mixing those two dubious sets of genes together, well it's little wonder that you ended up with someone like me emerging from the resultant genetic salad; I was an accident just waiting to fertilise.

Several months after my expulsion from Ravensbourne Boys School, my case was referred to a local doctor, who came and visited the house on a few occasions. He was old and musty and professorial, and I remember him peering at me over the top of his wire-framed spectacles, his eyes creasing up as they tried to bore into my very soul, or so it seemed. He asked me lots of probing questions and then sat there musing over the responses, his fingers knitting themselves into a little steeple as he did so. He seemed quite set on giving me something more concrete to go away with than anything that the Maudsley had thus far provided. A few weeks after his final visit my parents received a letter saying that he was fairly certain that I was 'educationally backward'; I think the word 'retarded' was bandied about too, but that term at least was fizzling out in professional circles and was instead becoming a word of opprobrium, and so 'educationally backward' it was. This dreadful diagnosis hung around on my medical records like a blot of greasy butter, and it would be well over a decade before a fresh sheet of paper and the correct diagnosis – autism – was duly considered. In the meantime, I was made to suffer all manner of forecasts of failure and portents of doom from this reprehensible old fart, who predicted that I would possibly amount to little more besides being packed off to a care home, where I might spend my days lolling back mindlessly in an armchair with a line of saliva dribbling down my chin, courtesy of some particularly potent medication. During a typical autistic meltdown on my part – several years down the line – this dubious diagnosis led to a heavy dose of Thorazine being administered in order to 'subdue' me. A couple of hours later I was rushed to hospital in an ambulance because I couldn't breathe; I was discharged the same day and then my throat seized up again, this time accompanied by the most violent, agonising convulsions centred around my neck and shoulders; back in the ambulance again, this time staying overnight until the effects of the drug wore off. I think I actually swallowed my tongue on that second occasion, but the recollection is understandably rather hazy.

Eventually I was placed at another senior school, this one several miles away from our house; two buses and a walk made the daily journey to Kemnal Manor Upper School (as it was then) a gruelling undertaking, but I threw myself into it with a certain amount of gusto, even agreeing to unearth my plimsolls and participate in the dreaded 'games' lessons. This was despite the fact that I still found the whole concept of 'games' utterly pointless, given that I'd already decided that I was going to be a writer and not a runner; meanwhile my ideal imaginary self – NT Me – seemed more settled on the idea of a City job, therefore insisting that I buckle down academically at once. In the end I fell afoul of yet another case of 'aggravated ableism', brawling on a bus after being taunted about my 'unusual' dyspraxic walk. I lost the fight, having vowed never to strike another human being ever again, on account of the awful expulsion experience back in junior school; I discovered on this occasion that there are only so many ways you can shove someone before they duck and then fell you with a sudden right, unfortunately. And so, my second senior school expulsion followed shortly thereafter, this one conducted mainly over the phone and through a series of hastily scribbled letters; cue a second period of house arrest, with conditions even stricter than before. I was 12 years old at the time. I was also utterly friendless, and the futile attempt I made at reconnecting with my oldest friend Simon Roberts fell flat on its face when I found out he'd gone and allied himself with some of my most demonstrative detractors back at Ravensbourne Boys School. I still hung around with my cousin Claire and a few of her friends but they were all girls and this caused me a few raised eyebrows from various quarters; the occasional boy joined the gang, but never really stuck around for very long. Being on occasion stereotypically cruel kids ourselves – I never said I was an angel – we used to make great sport of turning various local oddities into outright villains, like the clearly disabled man who lurched back and forth along the road at various points during the day, or even the poor old lady who lived next door, who I was quite convinced was a witch. Years later I vaguely made up for this questionable behaviour when I found her fallen over in her yard and was able to help her to her feet and back into the house; when it happened a second time I went and called the ambulance for her – who says that autistic people don't have any empathy?!? We have maybe way too much of it, if anything.

One final effort was made to send me to a 'normal' senior school. My parents and I were given an appointment by a sympathetic headmaster and I was taken to see the school in question (I've quite forgotten the name); we were escorted around the premises in a vaguely detached way by said headmaster, his manner reminiscent of the sort one might sport when perusing a telephone directory. However, when the other teachers were made aware of my rather dismal track record, I was refused a place pretty much on the spot. That was the end of my 'normal' education and the beginning of my rapid descent into the sordid pit of 1980s 'special needs' schools, or, as my mother called them back then, '…dumping grounds'. Being sent to a 'special needs' school was – back in the 1980s – the ultimate social shame, with much curtain-twitching and whispering amongst the neighbours when the rather sordidly nicknamed 'spag wagon' arrived at the house each morning to ferry you away. This was a minibus of some description, usually a bit battered and often emitting a rather noxious cloud of unnecessary fumes in its wake. Once inside you were strapped into your seat and told to keep your hands firmly by your sides. I remember sitting there in that minibus on that first day and looking from left to right, noting the nodding, lolling heads of my compatriots and the silvery lines of spittle dribbling down their chins, and then thinking to myself, Well you're at the bottom of the pot now, old boy. Not that I had anything against these poor kids, but I was clearly cut from a different cloth; they were perhaps staked out on the cruel, merciless end of the autistic spectrum, whereas I was an as-yet undiagnosed savant in the making. I would say that the general public has a pretty poor understanding of that particular end of the autistic spectrum – savants and the like – assuming that it can't be overly bothersome, whereas with me it had – and still has – a very profound effect on my day-to-day life.

I ended up running away the very next morning from this first special needs school – Foxley something-or-other – simply by absconding from the house shortly before the 'spag wagon' arrived. Unfortunately, I was spotted by the driver of the loathsome vehicle as it turned into the top of my road, engine spluttering and with those pungent exhaust fumes billowing out the back. I was hastily bustled on board, strapped down and off we went. On this occasion I was placed next to the attendant female teaching assistant/nurse/bouncer, a vision of brawny folded arms and furrowed monobrow, chewing gum and looking me up and down with a certain semi-professional disdain; 'This one's got trouble written all over his face,' she said to the driver, regarding my good self. She then turned back to me with a malicious gleam in her eye; 'I cut my milk teeth on troublemakers,' she sniffed, gently cracking her knuckles to punctuate the point.

I wasn't at Foxley something-or-other 'special needs' school for long and I've blacked most of it out of my mind simply on account of how awful it was. There was no teaching whatsoever and we were simply left to loll around, occasionally baking cakes or watching literally whatever we wanted on TV. You couldn't run away from the damned place because the fences were about ten feet high and also because they lurched backwards at the summit in order to prevent any effort at scaling them. One time one of the kids had a fit – and by this, I mean a temper tantrum/semi-autistic meltdown – and proceeded to wreck an entire classroom, hurling chairs about and the like. The teacher on duty at the time locked me in the room with him and then mouthed the words '…life lesson' at me through the square glass porthole of the door. I crouched down in a corner with my hands over my head until the tempest had subsided.

I don't recall any specific incident which led to my final expulsion – how could you get expelled from a place like that?!? – and most likely it was simply the fact of my parents pulling the plug on the whole wretched thing. However, on the basis of my alleged belligerence I was taken to task at the town hall by an assembly of some twenty or so 'officials', including the teacher who'd locked me in the room with that bad-tempered boy. Over the space of an hour or so they proceeded to perform a character assassination on me of quite the highest order, whilst I was encouraged to keep quiet and take it in the spirit in which it was intended; I was just twelve years old or so at the time. I remember scanning the room and then, at the end of my visual peregrinations, coming to the conclusion that I'd never before seen a bigger collection of a**** outside of the top shelf in the local newsagents in my entire life. Following on from this meeting, various threats were made to have me taken into care, and that particular threat was held over my head for several months/years like the Sword of Damocles, at least until my parents hit upon a more practical solution: the home tutor, a plan that would help rectify some of the yawning great gaps in my education.

Now, there are no words to describe how dire this man – Jim Alderson – was, in his tatty grey raincoat and with his drooping carroty moustache, not to mention his world-weary, socially inept wit. Like my Ravensbourne Boys School maths teacher Mr Clarke, Jim Alderson frequently enjoyed hitting me around the back of the head when I couldn't make head nor tail of my times-table; worse still, he also made fun of the way that I walked, doubtless having spied my liberal dash of dyspraxia. Just to reiterate, dyspraxia means that one's physical coordination and spatial awareness is poor; in my case, it made my gait in particular look somewhat…interesting/gawky…to say the least, for which I still hold those wretched callipers at least partly responsible. 'Jim' would sit there down one end of our living room with his arms folded and then encourage me walk towards him from the opposite end, simply so that he could have the pleasure of informing me that I '…walked like a spastic'. When the big hurricane of 1987 hit, I pretended that a stray gust of wind had knocked our doorbell out, allowing me to leave him stewing in the porch ahead of that day's particular lesson; I watched his discomfort with some small satisfaction from an upstairs window until he finally took the hint and ambled off. My dad wasn't too pleased about this – in fact his moral outrage was something to behold – but I was too kind and gracious to tell either of my parents just what a horror they'd hired. On his return the following day, 'Jim' let rip a terrible revenge by telling me that I would never have any friends on account of how weird I walked/talked/and so on and so forth. I nearly called him '…an old bastard!' in retaliation but feared too much the back of his hand once more around the side of my head. A few days later he performed the ultimate sin of making fun of my reading matter – mostly still vintage American comic books – and basically inferring that I must be as thick as two short planks if I enjoyed stuff like that. I retorted that I'd much rather bore my brain-cells with a bit of basic 'Batman' than by having to listen to any more of his shrewish carping, and certainly not by reading any of the sexually dubious paperbacks he frequently shoved under my nose. I can't remember whether or not he hit me for answering back so impertinently, but he most certainly would have called me a 'cretin' at least; that was his 'go-to' insult for anyone and anything he considered below his own pseudointellectual standard.

Besides 'Jim', I was also sent on a weekly basis to be tutored in maths by a woman who reeked of vinegar and who lived in a room piled high with stale-smelling old books. This lesson took place for an hour and a half every Friday evening, which meant missing the latest instalment of 'Cagney & Lacey'. I would stare at my watch for almost every single painful second of that hour and a half until she would catch me in the act, correcting me by lightly pinching the top of my hand until she left a little mark. There were also a couple more home tutors, but they were relatively mundane, especially when stood alongside the original carroty-moustached monster, 'Jim'. Apart from the occasional contact with my cousins, these were the only people with whom I interacted on a daily basis, but when you're that much of a social pariah – so I reasoned – then even being verbally or physically abused was human contact, of a sort.

A second 'special needs' school soon followed on from Foxley something-or-other. This one sported a considerably more relaxed regime, smaller class sizes and also the fact that I was alongside kids who, whilst troublesome, were bothered in a rather more benign fashion; also you got to make your way there and back under your own steam, which was a step up from the dreaded 'spag wagon'. There was still nothing to do once you got there, though, with every day turning into a complete and utter waste of time and energy; they didn't even teach me how to boil an egg, and by the time I turned fourteen I could honestly say that there were some kids living in Third World Countries who'd had a better bash at the education system than I'd ever had. My only consolation during these dark and dreary days were the TVAM strikes on ITV, which led to them running endless reams of the 60s 'Batman' series to paper over the broadcasting gaps; many were the bollockings I received for turning up late, all because I'd spent my mornings watching Julie Newmar camping it up in spandex. Well, it was either that or turning up at this latest 'special needs' school and spending seven hours staring out of a window towards an endless dreary green field and a horizon beyond that tinged with nothingness. What a complete and utter cock-up this whole period was – 'Batman' aside – and how I look back on it now as nothing less than a total failure of the 1980s education system in coping with even the basic needs of the neurodiverse.

Finally I was sent to a private school for about six months or so – The Coach House, which counted the formidable 'Jim' amongst its employees – a good distance away but speedily reached on the new white Racer bike I'd gotten for my birthday, allowing me to build up a rather tremendous pair of thighs in the process. It wasn't a proper private school, though; well, you had to pay to be taught there but it was filled with yet more misfits, although again rather more the benign sort, those perhaps with parents who actually gave marginally more of a stuff about them than was expected. These new classmates were academically adept but socially rather sterile; the odd cursory attempt at friendship was duly struck up between them and myself but nothing ever came of it. It was here at this private school that I got my one solitary GCSE, in English language. I considered that quite an achievement for someone who'd been called 'educationally backward' by peers, teachers and doctors alike. This whole time was a rather hazy one for me – the late 1980s – with this particular stint in the education system dated only by the fact of the Lockerbie air crash; one of the teachers at The

Coach House was an American and she was supposed to have been on this particular flight, but missed it for some unspecified reason. Her good fortune buoyed us up for an entire morning after the fact, but despite this she ended up losing her job several months later due to some undisclosed staff pruning measures, climbing the stairs to the classroom after being given her notice and sobbing her heart out on the little round table where we took our lessons. I remember how our little group of misfits looked on helplessly, trying as best as we could to comfort her, in our own socially awkward little ways.

'D' is for…

…developmental delay.

Monique Samuels was the first person to accurately spot what was really 'wrong' with me, the first person to discern that I wasn't where I should be developmentally, that in both educational and also emotional terms, things were 'delayed'. Basically, I guess she spied my 'spiky profile', which refers to the various areas of learning, excels rather drastically in some places whilst also failing dramatically in others, which I guess would seem pretty 'spiky' if you laid it out in a graph. She was also perhaps the first person to really talk to me like I mattered; the first person to react like my jokes really were funny, and like my opinions mattered, alongside all sorts of other vaguely intimidating 'grown-up' stuff. Monique was a youth worker at the Sight & Sound secretarial college on Charing Cross Road; the building is still extant but the shop below – back then a labyrinthine branch of Books Etc – is now a Primark or something. Up on the third floor she was tasked with reforming a motley crew of dissenting kids from the four corners of London, all of them sporting developmental delays of differing forms. It was Monique's task to metaphorically gob on these kids and then polish them up with a few swift strokes of her elbow, before then turning them back upon the world with renewed confidence, some good life-skills and a healthy dose of self-deprecating humour.

The life-affirming course that I found myself enrolled on lasted a little under three months, from October to December 1989, with an option to stay on to learn further office and secretarial skills if desired. Needless to say, NT Me was particularly pleased with the whole situation, and I myself was pretty pleased too; people were finally talking to me and not simply addressing the metaphorical 'spaz' sticker that school had plastered on my forehead for the last 11 years or so. It was an adventuresome but often arduous process, this gradual casting aside of my developmental delay and actually growing up. It's quite important to understand that this issue – growing up – is doubly difficult for an autistic person, many of whom as I think I've said, often retain a childlike outlook even when their faces have long since succumbed to gravity's relentless grab. One also has to factor in the 'problem' whereby many people persist in thinking that autism is a childhood condition, one that you shed as soon as you hit sixteen or something. But here I digress. At Sight & Sound I was, for the first time, mixing with people who were talking about sex and relationships and life in a properly adult way; even my older cousins tended only to cover these subjects in a sort of sniggered whisper of a conversation. Up until this point I'd also only ever met one black person (a bit of a bully, from Ravensbourne Boys School), but the Sight & Sound secretarial college was delightfully diverse, with peoples from a wide range of countries and cultures; for a boy brought up in the rather conservative, closed-up suburban streets of south-east London it was something of an eye-opener, to say the least. Monique herself was multiracial, originally from

Liverpool although in 1989 she was living in Leytonstone with her partner Peter and their dog – I think it was a Great Dane – called Shogun. When I first met her, I insisted on calling her 'Miss' constantly; it was an early indicator of the fact that whilst I'd moved on from school in terms of my age, I was still nevertheless firmly stuck there as far as my mind-set was concerned. This thinking would cement itself firmly in my psyche over the next few years, but at this point in time I was blissfully unaware of the damage that had been done by being excluded from school for so very long.

I remember Monique once telling me that various other members of staff had started teasing her where I was concerned; whenever I turned up in the big open-plan office on the first floor they would say 'There's Monique's favourite', or something similar. I quite liked that. Now that I was out there in the adult world, I was starting to realise that people fell into two distinct camps where my neurodiversity concerned; either they found my particular form of wide-eyed, occasionally insolent naiveté endearing, or else it turned them off entirely. At that point in my life I'd met so many of the latter that I'd come to the conclusion that I was some sort of a freak, but the indirect measures set in motion by Monique's sphere of influence slowly began swinging the pendulum the other way.

During my time at Sight & Sound, I also learnt the various ins and outs, the dos and don'ts of daily commuting to London. I have to stress that London circa 1989 was a very different beast to the vaguely sanitised tourist trap it is today; back then there were still porno cinemas to be glimpsed up the side streets on and around Piccadilly Circus, and newsstands still sold similar magazines quite flagrantly. As my bus pulled to a halt at the traffic lights just before Piccadilly, I would look to my left and get a real good aerial view of the various titles on offer, all boobs and biceps galore; it was quite disturbing to such an artless and callow little creature as myself. You also saw homeless people everywhere, particularly in the dingy subway that connected part of Charing Cross Road to Tottenham Court Road Underground; here they were literally piled up in stacks to the left and to the right, although I soon learnt that it was bad form to simply stop and stare. Also, the various gay bars dotted around Old Compton Street and down St. Martin's Lane had for the most part blacked-out windows; I once asked a passer-by why this was the case, to which the rather harried-looking businessman replied, 'So we don't all have to lose our lunches if we happen to peer inside.' When I stuck my head into the bar of the Brief Encounter bar on St. Martin's Lane, however, all the clientele were doing was drinking, gossiping and smoking, crowded around the one stately old queen, who was busily regaling the bar staff with various tales and anecdotes that drew either howls of laughter or snorts of derision from his audience, captive or otherwise.

During my early London days I also learned to find my way around the aforementioned Underground, and rode almost all of the London Bus routes that went out of Victoria Station, with a particular penchant for the no.38; the no. 38 passed down Charing Cross Road and was thus convenient for the Sight & Sound college. At the very end of the route, the no.38 then ended up in Leytonstone. This was handy because Monique had taken such a shine to me that she actually invited me over to her house one Saturday afternoon, sometime during late 1989; we took Shogun for a walk in the park, went shopping and also discussed the merits of 'Naf Naf' fashion for a white boy more used to wearing C & A. She also explained to me gently that I simply couldn't go around saying the first thing that popped into my head, and that many people would get upset if I carried on like this. This was the first time someone that had pointed out to me in a reasoned manner the fact that I didn't 'do' dialogue like a neurotypical. Shortly after this, Monique confirmed her suspicions and sent me off to a psychiatrist, one who dutifully and swiftly diagnosed autism; if only someone had taken such care and attention when I was still in school, I might have salvaged some of my education. Unfortunately, it was to take several years – and some hard battling on the part of my parents – before the wording of my new diagnosis was changed on an official level, which meant several more years with the misdiagnosis of 'educationally backward' hanging over me like a cartoon raincloud. In the meantime, I began work on amending my idioms, which meant in the first instance apologising to fellow classmate Omiros for telling him in no uncertain terms that running away from home and then sleeping on the streets meant that he smelled. Now, I felt doubly bad about this because Omiros had been good enough to help me carry home a new record player all the way from Tottenham Court Road to my house, sometime in December 1989. I'd sent him packing afterwards without so much as a cup of tea or a digestive biscuit; the little social courtesies of life often pass one by when one is autistic.

Under Monique's ministrations I soon found myself holding conversations quite adequately, although another classmate, Louise, remarked that talking with me in those early days was a bit like '…talking to someone who was being attacked by bees.' Despite this I clicked quite well with my classmates during those three months at the fag-end of 1989. In fact, Monique often had to separate Louise and I, given our tendency to get the giggles whenever we were within eyeshot; this peaked during a visit to the Charing Cross Library, where Monique was forced to administer a severe dressing-down to the pair of us in full view of the staff member who'd been so kind in showing us around. Louise was lovely, but a little volatile; perhaps she'd been sent to Monique so that Monique might hone down a few of those rougher edges, as I've said.

Monique wasn't always taking us to various places of business in order to show us just how industry worked, however; one time we all visited the big HMV near Oxford Circus, to see Terrence Trent D'arby perform live from his new album 'Neither fish nor flesh' – it flopped, but everyone seemed to be thrilled to see him, at least before the sales figures rolled in. Despite her dismay at the juvenile behaviours that Louise and I often exhibited, Monique had a mischievous sense of humour that I found entirely compatible with my own, and I was certainly complicit when she drew her lipstick on poor Omiros as he dozed away in a Piccadilly Line tube carriage, on the way back from Heathrow. She also found it quite hilarious that I used the word 'shan't' when it came to wiggling out of things I didn't particularly want to do; 'I shan't go there!'; 'You shan't make me!' and so on and so forth. She would repeat what I'd say and then really enunciate the words she found amusing, until she was literally 'rolling in the aisles' with laughter. I think at times my autism made me a rather amusing prospect for people and that was perfectly fine by me; it certainly made a change from the outright vehemence I'd encountered in school. In fact, being showered with the occasional outpouring of panegyric was rather pleasing. This doesn't mean that I couldn't find myself occasionally overcompensating for the fact that the Sight & Sound office provided me with an all-but semi-captive audience; many was the time I leant against the doorway of the admin section, extolling the praises of the latest issue of 'Smash Hits' or 'Number One', only to find the recipient of my fervour glazing over with Olympian weariness. What I guess I'm trying to say is that it's not true that autistic people are poor social mixers; sometimes you can't get them to shut up for toffee. It's all about the topic, totally.

During my time at Sight & Sound I learnt a skill which would stand me in almost as great a stead as actually being officially diagnosed with autism; I learned how to type, and how to type pretty damn fast, at that. I was sat with several other people in what seemed to be a soundproofed room, with this big screen full of flashing letters suspended on the far wall directly ahead of us. We all had keyboards and we would hit the letters on our keyboards that corresponded with those being flashed up on that big screen. At the same time as the letters flashed up, a deep, monotone voice would repeat them out loud, sort of like this: 'A now, F now, C now, H now...' and so on and so forth, over and over and over and over again. I suppose it was a sort of brainwashing, but it sure as hell worked; I can still hit around 70wpm now if I'm totally in the zone, my hands sometimes moving so fast that they become a sort of blur – and they say you can't teach an autistic dog new tricks. In fact, I'm pretty sure that you could train an autistic person to perform almost any given task just like a neurotypical, if you hit them with it in a similar fashion; you could train them to maintain perfect eye contact during a conversation, for instance, although whether you should have to train them to behave just a like a neurotypical is another matter entirely. My dreaded dyspraxia reared its head during these initial touch-typing lessons; my hands didn't fly over the keyboard the way that they were supposed to, rather individual digits sort of darted out like little baby birds grabbing for food. One of the teachers pulled me up on this, but she was at least kind enough not to grab my wrist and then actually force me to try typing in the 'correct' manner. To that end, I still type in this strange 'off-touch' way to this very day, but as I said, it hasn't impaired my actual speed or accuracy one little bit.

My placement officer at Sight & Sound sent me for several job interviews during early 1990; this was Monique's rather more formal sister Maxine, and however hard she tried, well, I never managed to hold down any of the positions she attempted to secure for me. I worked for about five minutes as a teaching assistant at a kid's school somewhere out near Notting Hill, but they 'let me go' because the noise the kids made meant that I spent most of the time stood there with my hands clamped over my ears, fighting back against full sensory overload. I then got a job working weekday mornings in a Dunkin' Doughnuts just off Piccadilly Circus, although I barely lasted one day before I'd been sacked for squeezing the entire contents of a syrup bottle all over a belligerent customer's order. In a career move unrelated to Maxine's efforts, I also began working mornings at a nearby gym where I'd been trying to build some muscle, just off the Tottenham Court Road. The guy who ran the place – Fabrice – offered me free membership on top of a basic starter wage, and all I had to do was open up the place for him every morning and then mind the store for a few hours; every morning from 7am, otherwise known in normal lingo as 'stupid o'clock'. I think I lasted about a fortnight before I almost fainted with fatigue. It was sort of weird, his entrusting the place to me without me even having to fill in a form; what a fabulous time the late 80s/early 90s really was, back before the minutiae of human life began being logged on a daily basis. Anyway, the situation at the gym wasn't helped by the fact that I fell asleep under one of the sunbeds and woke up looking like your average pasty Brit after their first excursion to Magaluf. A day or so later I made my sincerest apologies to Fabrice, that I would perhaps be better off trusting to the fickle whims of fate where my physique was concerned, and that he might be better entrusting the place to a person with perhaps a modicum of common sense. Whilst I was there, he'd also tried to teach me how to eat healthier too – rice and noodles and such-like – but with two Burger Kings directly opposite each other on that little corner of the nearby Tottenham Court Road, well, he was pretty much onto a loser from the get-go.

During my time at Sight & Sound, Margaret Thatcher's highly unpopular Poll Tax set off the riots which occurred on Saturday 31st March 1990. I myself barely had any comprehension of politics back then; I could only ever recall Mrs Thatcher being prime minister, so the fact that – for starters – she was a woman was no big deal for me. People always said that she was a '…brute', but really, I couldn't see it; she always looked so well turned-out. As for the Labour Party, well the only thing that had ever gotten me excited about them up to that point was the fact that Michael Foot was almost a dead ringer for William Hartnell, the first 'Doctor Who'. No, I was a 'Thatcher's child' to all intents and unintentional purposes, and my parents had always voted Conservative, at least as far as I was then aware.

Anyway, I can't remember exactly what it was that I was doing on that particular Saturday in question, but most likely I was riding the various buses in and out of Victoria Station – hello no.38 – sat upstairs at the back and reading through my latest harvest of comic books, courtesy of Forbidden Planet. I wasn't in Trafalgar Square initially but at some point I ended up nearby, at the bottom of Charing Cross Road; the riots were spilling up into the rest of the West End and people were looting the various music shops on Charing Cross Road and also Denmark Street, site of the famous 'Tin Pan Alley'. The Sight & Sound building was situated just around the corner from Denmark Street and already several of the windows had been cracked; nearby, people were actually breaking the windows of various music shops and then simply climbing in, helping themselves to trombones and guitars and plenty of other expensive stuff besides. I called Monique from the phone box directly across the road and she in turn called the manager, Jeffrey Keen; she thought I was winding her up at first, such was the nature of our banter; 'I shan't lie to you!' I think I declared to her. I then set off in the direction of Trafalgar Square, thinking that perhaps I might pick up the no.24 bus outside South Africa House, which would then take me back to Victoria. Instead I found myself right in the thick of the action, bearing witness to the now-famous footage of the horses charging and the rioters throwing bits of barriers and placards at them, with one man getting totally trampled in the process. Back up Charing Cross Road I went, detouring down Denmark Street and pausing for breath on the cusp of St Giles High Street, with the Centre Point 'skyscraper' looming directly overhead; 'Come in here!!' someone hollered. When I turned to see where the voice was coming from, I found myself confronted with a row of fraught, anxious faces pressed up against the window of a small café on the dingy far corner of St Giles High Street. One of the waiters, a tall, gangly guy in a white pinny, pranced over and practically pulled me inside with a dramatic arc of his arm, telling me that I should wait out 'the riot' with the rest of his clientele. I politely declined his offer, reclaimed my limb and then quickly went on my way. I got as far as those fountains in front of the Centre Point 'skyscraper', with just enough time to finish off my comics, before dipping down into that dingy subway that ran toward Tottenham Court Road Underground, before emerging out the other side, at the bottom of Oxford Street. I witnessed more scenes of looting around the corner of Soho Street, with people climbing in through shattered shop windows and emerging seconds later with their arms full of stolen stock; for one brief moment I thought…should I?...before my conscience kicked in and I sought refuge in the nearby Virgin Megastore – now long since vanished – on the bottom corner of Oxford Street, turning into Tottenham Court Road. I saw Kim Wilde in there once and I blew her a kiss; she reciprocated, and I was made up pretty much for the rest of that day. Regarding the Poll Tax troubles though, well, I learnt a valuable social lesson that day that stayed with me forever;

peaceful protests get nowhere, but violent riots always get results.

*

I left Sight & Sound around July 1990; further attempts at securing me a placement with companies as wide-ranging as John Lewis and British Airways met with little success, and really there was nowhere else left for me to go as far as the college's employment scheme was concerned. I kept in touch with Monique for a couple of years, but I think in the end she went back to Liverpool and had the family she always seemed so keen on starting up. I've sought her out online several times over the years but have shied away from making any sort of direct contact. I have much, much to thank her for, but I worry she'll remember me simply as that rather mischievous, slightly eccentric little lad who harboured a deep, sometimes almost pathological dislike of the schools in which he'd suffered such ignominies, and little else besides. I never saw Louise or Omiros again (I have a vague memory of bumping into the latter at Victoria Station in the early 90s, but it's hazy; I was clearly in my clubbing phase at the time, whereas he painfully wasn't), but I did hang around with a Jewish girl from our group called Helena for several years, before we too drifted apart. I think I became a sort of surrogate boyfriend for her, although she was maybe nine or ten years older than myself, making her something of an anomaly amongst our little gathering of teenaged tearaways. I met up with her recently in the hope of reigniting some of my more frayed neurodiverse neurons, but it simply wasn't the same; she was older still, and a little wearier with it. I have, however, kept all of the notes we used to pass each other in class, pages and pages of them, in fact, most of it complete and utter rot, but vaguely touching all the same. Nowadays I'm actually more in touch with some of my old tutors from Sight & Sound more than I am with any of my actual classmates; it's almost as though some of those kids have all but vanished from the face of the earth. I've looked and looked for them on Facebook, but I can't find even the slightest trace; perhaps the girls got married and their names changed, that's all I can think of. But still, it really is like they all simply just vanished into the ether. I like to think that they all 'made it' though, somehow or other. We were all of us troubled, and it took some of us a little longer to 'come good' than it did the others, but I like to think they're still out there somewhere, and that occasionally they look back on those sunny Sight & Sound days with a smile. I know that I certainly do.

'E' is for…

…extreme behaviour.

Or in this particular case, extremist behaviour; enter Nicky Crane, notorious neo-Nazi and scourge of South London. When I met him, he was actually just a rather robustly reformed doorman, apologising profusely to various colleagues for the 'I hate n******' tattoos on his biceps, eking out a living guarding the Golden Lion pub in Soho, the dive where serial killer Dennis Nilsen snared several of his victims. I had 'prior' with Nilsen from when I was maybe 7 or 8, visiting the Forbidden Planet comic shop on Denmark Street while my dad drank and read the Daily Mail nearby; said shop was almost directly opposite Nilsen's place of work at the Denmark Street Jobcentre. Nilsen's puppy 'Bleep' ran across the road – apparently, he took her to work with him on occasion – and jumped up on my leg. I spent the next five minutes regaling Nilsen with my 'Amazing Spiderman' comics, until he realised that I was perhaps too tender a prospect to be procured and then throttled, then stashed away for future perusal beneath his floorboards. I regaled Nicky Crane with this anecdote as he sat at his little table by the Golden Lion's front door, doing The Times crossword; he smiled and then rolled his eyes in acknowledgement at my apparent good fortune.

Nicky Crane was quite a hard person to talk to – and coming from an autistic person that's really saying something – because, despite his rep, he was in person really rather quiet and soft-spoken. His piercing blue eyes tended to do a lot of the talking for him, actually, flashing with amusement or irritation alternately, depending on the company he was keeping. As I said, he was also quite self-conscious about his tattoos; I think I might have been too, if I were plastered with politically incorrect, downright offensive slogans almost from head to toe. But yes, he could indeed be overly apologetic about them if he happened upon a black person who quite naturally took offence at the sight; the artwork sporting the aforementioned awful word springs readily to mind. There was another doorman, a big black guy called Jay, who worked in Comptons, just around the corner from the Golden Lion, down nearby Old Compton Street. He knew Nicky by sight and Nicky was always apologising to him in regard to his tattoos, clamping his paws over them whenever he walked past the doorway to Comptons. I also became pretty good friends with Jay, too. We used to go to the big arcade around the corner on Wardour Street, spending hours trying to top our high scores on the various machines; sometimes we'd get quite a crowd gathered as we co-piloted some imaginary spaceship or other, or else tried to push our respective cars off the road in some garishly fast racing game. I later heard that Dennis Nilsen also used to scope out that particular arcade as another potential point for picking up his victims, but by then he'd been behind bars for at least eight years or so, saving me the misfortune of a perhaps more perilous second encounter.

It was around this time that I also made the acquittance

of pop journalist and Guardian columnist Richard Smith and his boyfriend Michael; they took me to see 'The Krays', my first ever 'grownup' movie, as well as chaperoning me on my first Pride march, back when it was more political and less prancing; they also spent a great deal of time trying to talk me out of 'hanging around' with a character like Nicky Crane. One time, Richard had cut out a piece from an anti-fascist magazine, sliding it across the Formica surface of the table in the café in which we were dining, his finger firmly on the grainy black and white of Nicky Crane's head; 'Your lovely friend,' he said, with a dubiously raised eyebrow.

'But why would he do all that?' I asked, peering at the particulars of the article.

'Because he's a thug.'

'…a thug and a racist,' Michael interjected.

'What's a racist?' I asked.

Richard scoffed. 'Mickey, didn't you go to school?!'

At this point I think I coloured considerably. 'Well, not much, no…' and then I smiled. 'He's really, really nice, though! I could introduce you, if you like!'

'You'll do no such thing, young man!' Richard snapped, and that was the end of that.

The idea of Nicky Crane as a friend – of sorts – took my fancy because he was imposing, menacing, covered in tattoos, a semi-'celebrity', and therefore totally unlike anything I'd ever encountered thus far in my 16 or so years on the planet. To be perfectly frank he was a freak, just like me, although he'd taken the pains to have the fact painted all over him, whereas I could still 'pass' for 'normal' if I kept perfectly still and didn't speak. I therefore made it my business to inveigle myself into Nicky Crane's world as best I could, keeping the fact a shameful secret from Richard and Michael whenever I saw them. Now, being autistic and trying to make friends with someone presented itself as a considerable difficulty, but because I was young and 'cute' I readily allowed the strange freemasonry of the men frequenting the Golden Lion to perform the necessary overtures on my part. Pretty soon I was popping round to Nicky Crane's flat on nearby Rupert Street on a regular basis, pressing the buzzer at the door on the street and then peering up at the third-floor window as his formidable head and shoulders loomed over the sill to see who it was. The flat itself was fairly claustrophobic, but back then I considered the notion of living in the very centre of Soho to be a major coup; now I think perhaps I'd rather stick hot needles in my eyes. There was a big framed picture of Ronnie Kray on the wall opposite the window, alongside pictures of Nicky himself, all of them cultivated from various newspaper cuttings; a particularly scathing piece from The Sun had pride of place overlooking his bed, with the headline 'Nazi Nick is a panzi!' *(sic)*. Looking back, I think he was quite taken with his own rather tumultuous little stamp upon the world. I used to bring various videos with me on my visits and we'd watch them together, but never anything particularly highbrow; I wasn't particularly highbrow back then, to be honest. I'm not particularly highbrow now, come to think of it, but I can 'pseudointellectual' with the best of them. I remember that he quite liked 'Batman Returns', so that dates that particular visit to sometime during late 1992 or early 1993. I also remember that he had a documentary on the Krays that I really wanted to watch, and that I pestered him about it until finally he gave in, jamming the thing into the video recorder with a clearly audible tut. You see, he was the perfect gentleman, but there was, I felt, a terrible temper lurking just beneath that courtly demeanour.

I also went on several occasions to visit him at St. Mary's Hospital in Paddington, whenever he got ill from the AIDS virus that was slowly doing away with him. That first visit to St. Mary's was a lesson in the horror of human mortality, something that hadn't really struck me when various of my grandparents had died. I never knew my father's father, but I was rather fond of my paternal grandmother, who was always jamming her silver change into my hand whenever she thought no one else was watching. My maternal grandmother died when I was fairly young but I do remember her, especially the stultifying boredom of an afternoon at her house during the summer holidays, when I was very young and when my mum was out at work; 'When is my mum coming to get me?' I would ask her, usually at five-minute intervals.

'Presently,' she would say, quite calmly, hands folded in her lap.

'Yeah, but how long is "presently"?' I would persist.

'Presently,' she would reply, a little more firmly, now.

'Yeah, but how many hours and how many minutes is that, exactly?!'

And on and on it would go.

Her husband, my maternal grandfather, lived on well after she died and used to come to our house for tea, every Tuesday I think it was; they only lived four doors down from us, meaning that my mum had effectively lived in the same road her entire life. 'Grandad Whitebread' used to bring me a sweet every Tuesday, usually a ghastly thing called a 'honeycomb', which left my teeth looking as though I'd gargled from a pot of gold paint. I don't remember much more about him other than the fact that he looked a little like the vintage horror actor Boris Karloff, and that he would walk around with his hands clasped firmly behind his back, the way that Prince Phillip often did when making public appearances.

Anyway, the first time I went to St. Mary's to see Nicky Crane was late in the evening on a Monday or a Tuesday, circa 1992 or maybe 1993. The Rodney Porter ward in which I found myself was quite dark and labyrinthine; in fact, to my suggestible mind it seemed to be lit in an almost deliberately morbid manner. I crept along past various open doors and saw pale, gaunt faces peering back at me out of the darkness; one of them smiled as I paused on the threshold, whether out of wry amusement at my anxiety or as some sort of signal to conversation and company, I don't know. I'm ashamed to say I didn't linger long enough to find out. I went and found Nicky Crane's room and then I spent the next hour or so trying my best to take his mind off what was happening to him. As I remember it now I rather imagine myself sitting there reading Mein Kampf aloud to him, reciting the awful text in a manner to remind him of the horrors of his previous life, but to tell you the truth I more likely entertained him with tales from the various comic books I collected; I think maybe Richard Smith had snorted the Mein Kampf thing as a derisory joke when I told him about my charitable venture. On one of these visits, Nicky wondered aloud if he would be able to see his own funeral when it was happening, whether he would be hovering in the sky directly above it, like a ghost, I guess. As I've said, I was still too young and too unawares of the realities of mortality to understand the entirety and then the sudden cessation of someone else's life, so I wasn't quite sure how to respond. I remember his voice kind of cracked when he told me that he had cancer; again, I was totally ignorant of how such awful conditions could sidle into the human body, even as it fought against the other indiscriminate ravages of AIDS. I think I tried to change the subject by asking him his thoughts about Doctor Hans Asperger being a Nazi, but I really don't recall how he responded; probably he was by that point past caring about such trivialities. The fact that Doctor Asperger might have been a Nazi seems now to have become a source of great concern for the neurodiverse community. I guess if they decide that he was a Nazi after all then it means that they will have to disown him, the way Americans seem to be disowning their pasts by tearing down statues of racist generals. Then I guess the 'aspies' will have to start calling themselves something else. I shan't mind.

I was never entirely sure what Nicky Crane actually made of me attaching myself to his life limpet-style, but perhaps he felt a vague kind of kinship with someone who seemed to be as much of an outsider as he perhaps was. When I wasn't with Nicky and when I wasn't being lectured for being with Nicky by Richard, well then I was hanging about with a veritable smorgasbord of disreputable characters, all of whom I knew from the pubs and arcades around the Soho/Charing Cross Road area, close stomping grounds to my former base of salvation at Sight & Sound. One of these characters was a young lad called Vincent, who became my best friend for about a year; we went on daring expeditions to seedy pubs in faraway Docklands, and I distinctly remember on one occasion having to rub baby oil over him in an amateur strip competition when no one else from the audience deigned to do him the pleasure. He lived in Willesden, which might as well have been another world to me; he always used to tell me that the black boys living around there would make mincemeat of me. I never bothered to respond by telling him that I'd just enrolled at a youth training scheme in Hackney and was already adjusting my tongue's suburban twang to something a little more 'street' in order to acclimatise. I even owned a couple of pairs of 'Hammer pants' back then, when they were fashionable; 'Hammer pants' were baggy great balloon things that did nothing for your arse whatsoever, but they were what 'MC Hammer' wore and he was all the rage for about five minutes during the early 1990s, and thus so were his misshapen trousers.

Before joining that youth training scheme in Hackney, I was briefly enrolled as a student at Islington Itec, in a glistening brown-brick building on Rosebery Avenue, not far from the big Mount Pleasant post office. This was from about January to March 1991, and I didn't last long there because even the most basics of IT were utterly beyond my illogical mind. In fact, I take my hat off to myself simply for making it several months on the premises, given that I didn't have a clue what computers were all about; I thought a 'spread-sheet' was something you took with you on a picnic. There was a black girl at Islington Itec called Denise, who was a bit gobby and who on one occasion got into something of a row with our redheaded classmate Brad. As a result, she got her 'gangsta' brother to wait outside for him – he was a friend, of sorts – and this much older, bigger man stood there waiting for Brad in a sort of vaguely intimidating pose as we left the premises, just a pair of pale, innocent white boys doing their best not to appear nonplussed. We turned a right up Rosebery Avenue, heading towards High Holborn, at which point Brad told me to 'just keep walking' and not to look back. I couldn't for the life of me see what we'd done wrong, not considering the fact that Denise was the one with the big gob to begin with, but there you go. Anyway, despite her trying her best to set her big brother on us, nothing actually happened; perhaps he was just a 'plastic gangster'.

As for Vincent, well, he was adopted, for one thing; he had no siblings and even his adopted parents didn't seem to be in the picture when I first met him. He wanted very much to be loved but he ended up being a rent boy instead, at which point we sort of lost touch; that lifestyle was a bit too extreme, even for me. One time he 'bagged' a celebrity punter and used the spoils to buy me a slap-up meal, before taking us both to see 'Fried Green Tomatoes at the Whistle Stop Café' in Leicester Square; twenty pounds went a long way in those days, not including the celebrity punter's tip. Despite these and other occasional kindnesses, he still attempted to yank me along on his one-way voyage into the sexual abyss, but I pulled back after encountering a glut of rent boys in the Golden Lion and hearing one of them exclaim, in regard to myself, 'She thinks she's it, she does!' – Well I certainly had 'Hammer pants', if nothing else.

We both loved Madonna, Vincent and I. We pored over her pictures, went and saw her mostly dire movies, and tried to behave for the most part like her semi-dissolute character 'Susan' in 'Desperately Seeking Susan', which was the only really decent picture she ever made. 'Susan' lived hand-to-mouth and relied on her streetwise savvy to see her through life; she behaved more like a man, basically. In lieu of getting caught up in a search for some lost Egyptian earrings, we made do attending Nicky Crane's birthday party, where TV cook Rustie Lee tried teaching me to laugh in the same tenor as her cacophonous Caribbean pitch. We also tried selling a story to The Sun about a famous 1980s DJ I met in a Soho bar, where he tried to bribe me into visiting his house in Islington, mostly by offering to buy me lots of original American comic book artwork, of which he was a prodigious collector. A week or so later Vincent and I met a reporter from the aforementioned newspaper and furnished him with all of the relevant details. Several days after that I got cold feet, following a sudden premonition about seeing my face plastered all over the national newspapers, perhaps linked in some tentative way to a sordid Soho rent boy clique. In a vaguely creepy twist, this DJ was years later actually investigated in regard to some sort of a grooming scandal, but from what I can remember he wasn't prosecuted. In fact, he was never anything but courteous and kind to me and I still feel like a bit shitty when I think of how close we came to 'outing' his predilection for teenage boys. The age of consent was kind of archaic back then, whereas now I don't think he'd find himself in much hot water at all.

At other times Vincent and I hung around with a mixed-race rent boy called Ben, who'd been effectively abandoned by his family in much the same way as Vincent had. Ben's entire life revolved around the pubs and bars in

Soho and he even had a flat on the corner of Rupert Street and Tisbury Court, said corner being where all of the prostitutes and their pimps hung out. I remember the sun pouring in the through the windows of this high-ceiled, airy domicile whilst down below Soho life continued as normal, with Nicky Crane sometimes leaning out of his window opposite and surveying the proceedings with an airy disdain. It was obviously quite a coup to have a Soho flat, but I was a bit troubled by Ben, sprawled face-down on one occasion on his big white bed and sobbing his heart out at the empty life he was leading; he seemed to me to be a world away from Nicky Crane's carefully constructed Soho 'celebrity' bubble. Years later, the restaurant/café Vegan Hippo would do a brisk trade just below what were once the windows to Ben's flat, out of which I'd peered so innocently. I didn't know what a vegan was back then either, the same way that I was blissfully ignorant of cancer as it attacked Nicky Crane as part of his AIDS ordeal, but both subjects would rear their heads with particularly unpleasant consequences for me in the years to come.

Nicky Crane died sometime in the early 1990s; I went to his funeral and listened to Mariah Carey's song 'Hero' booming out over the speakers as the service finished. I guess on reflection he was a hero, of sorts; to work yourself up into a white supremacist lather as neo-Nazi before realising how wrong you'd been and then publicly apologising for the fact at every given opportunity certainly took some guts. I know that's probably a cold comfort to some of the people he crossed during his misspent youth, but at least he tried to turn himself around. This didn't wash with Richard Smith though, even though Richard was a hero to me too, precisely because he'd spent his life battling against the bigotry of people like Nicky Crane. It's strange how intolerant the tolerant are.

As for poor Vincent, well, he ended up dead too, after

having caught AIDS from some ghastly punter, or else perhaps from a night of fleeting passion with someone who cared about him for roughly five minutes or so; Ben told me about it several years after the fact when I bumped into him in Trafalgar Square. I couldn't bring myself to imagine what a cold and meagre affair Vincent's funeral might have been, or how dank and overgrown his grave might be now, or even if he has one. But maybe he had secret pockets in his life of which I was completely unawares, and there are other people who still remember him to this day; the whole world doesn't revolve around me, although when one has autism your general inclination is to think that it does.

'F' is for…

…fine motor skills (or the lack thereof).

You might be able to spot an autistic person simply because their hand and eye movements are sometimes a little out of sync; on this basis they might do 'dad dancing' several decades earlier than they ought to, and if – when map reading – they say 'go right' but then point left, well it might be best to ask them to verify, just in case. This isn't to be disparaging; it's simply a fact, and I have on occasion been about as 'out of sync' as it's possible to get. It's simply an observation, with a wry comment or two thrown in to try and lighten the mood a little. You can either be bogged down in the dreary details of autism, or you can try and shine a little humour and a little positivity on them; laugh and the world laughs with you, and all that.

Circa 1991/2 I reckon most lads my age would have been content with hanging around in a youth club, or simply standing on the nearest available street corner, sneering disparagingly at passers-by. Because I was autistic, I was busily seeking out likeminded 'social lepers', of which the mean streets of early 90s London offered a virtual profusion. At some point, my search led me to begin attendance at the 'London Connection' drop-in centre, located not far from Trafalgar Square. This place was run mainly for the benefit of the hordes of homeless youth that congregated around the West End of London, especially on The Strand. Now I wasn't homeless in any way, shape or form, but the staff seemed to simply assume that I was a rent-boy or something, albeit one fortunate enough to have a bed for the night (I was always well turned-out), even if that bed was – in their minds – the rather unwelcome abode of some greedily pawing punter. I was happy to facilitate this façade with the odd coy comment, mainly because renting seemed at that somewhat naïve stage of my life – and via Vincent's hyperbole – a rather glamourous occupation, to be the sought-after sexual plaything of the rich and the powerful. If pressed upon for the details of my trade, I would simply regale the staff with tales of the time a prominent Tory MP had once winked at me from across a relatively empty bar in Piccadilly Circus. When he then decided to hang around outside said bar and wait for me, well, that was another matter entirely and I was forced to hide in the disabled toilet until I was sure he'd gone. On top of this there was also the whole 1980s DJ episode to consider, but I don't really recall flashing that one about too much in order to heighten my illicit lustre. Maybe the staff and users of the London Connection also assumed that I was some sort of streetwalker because I'd namedropped Nicky Crane several times; the Golden Lion was a notorious rent boy haunt, after all. A stocky lesbian skinhead called Jackie once tried to pimp me from the premises and then threatened to do me bodily harm if I disobeyed, but Nicky Crane had a quiet word with her, and she promptly took her 'services' elsewhere.   One of the workers at the 'London Connection', using considerably more colourful language than Richard Smith, went to great pains to point out to me that Nicky Crane was a '…f***ing Nazi', this even after I'd told them all about Rustie Lee attending Nicky Crane's birthday party. But maybe with my strange gawky gait and my 'compromised' fine motor skills, perhaps the London Connection staff simply saw straight through me from the start, discerning someone maybe a mere stone's throw from a dirty blanket on the Strand for reasons besides renting, and so they let me stay on that count. I ended up staying four years in all, including excursions to the Forest of Dean (twice), Glastonbury and Alton Towers. We also went to the cinema several times, and sometimes even enjoyed an afternoon at the theatre. For these West End shows it was normally a 'charitable' act via the manager to give us a stub of free tickets, as they sought to pack out their empty pews; we would dutifully sit through whatever crap it was that the rest of the West End didn't much care for, scoffing popcorn and occasionally hurling it around, normally whenever the business on the stage became that bit too boring.

When we went to Glastonbury, we stayed in a big farmhouse alongside a series of rolling hills, but still close to the town, whereas both Forest of Dean excursions were to a more secluded residence, many miles from civilisation. Shared cooking and cleaning chores were compulsory, and these tasks certainly taught me a few valuable life lessons that I hadn't picked up at home, courtesy of my overindulgent mother. I shared a room with a lad my age who snored like a trumpet; despite waking him several times in the night he persisted, so the next morning I filled his shoes with shaving foam in a moment of bleary-eyed revenge. I got bawled out by one of the London Connection workers for doing that, a shock considering it came from a gentle soul called Clarence, who was pretty much the most amiable person you could possibly hope to meet. Still, it was my bad and so I took the punishment on the chin. Later, with my conscience fully salved, I was able to join in the chorus of disapproval when another unpopular lad was slighted by having a rusty anvil secreted in the bottom of his rucksack.

The London Connection youth group met in a big hall adjacent to St-Martin-in-the-Fields, every Thursday evening, from 6 until 9pm. The staff remained fairly consistent throughout my tenure, all of them totally tolerant of this procession of broken little kids who came capering through their doors every week. They helped them with their washing and sometimes sought to fix them up with more permanent accommodation, something considered a vital first step on the path back to social respectability. I first learnt about political correctness at the London Connection and – as an extension of my time with Monique – I had it drummed into me yet again that you couldn't simply go around saying this or that without there being some sort of consequence. It didn't matter to the staff that I was neurodiverse or that I had difficulty walking in a straight line; if I was self-aware enough to know what I was, then I was also self-aware enough to keep it in check, if and when social circumstances dictated. I received several sound verbal warnings for my conduct over the years, and I have to say it narked me that the staff were always so tolerant of everyone else but rarely of me and my clearly obvious 'condition'. A couple of times I was even barred from turning up on a Thursday evening, but I can count on the fingers of one hand the amount of times this rather extreme measure was taken. Having autism doesn't necessarily make you a potty-mouthed little beast incapable of distinguishing good manners from bad; instead, it merely cajoles you into spitting out the alleged slur several seconds before your vaunted 'high functioning' self has gotten a handle on it.

I first heard about the London Connection whilst hanging around with the various ageing social misfits who collected around the Kentucky Fried Chicken 'restaurant' at Marble Arch. Some of these guys – I hate calling them 'odds and sods' but really, that's that they were – ranted and railed at Speaker's Corner every Sunday, a stone's throw over the road from the KFC in Hyde Park. The name of the guy who actually directed me to the London Connection was Rob, but at the KFC and over on Speaker's Corner people instead called him 'Page Boy'; this nickname involved an anecdote that I, being too self-involved at the time, was unable to properly digest. He was bespectacled and bucktoothed but as I was myself 'disabled', beggars basically couldn't be choosers, at least not where making photogenic friends was concerned. We weren't really friends for very long but he did tell me about the London Connection and for some reason it sounded right up my alley, somewhere to pass the time when I wasn't niggling Nicky Crane, vamping it up with Vincent, or else being railed at by Richard Smith. Like me, 'Page Boy' had problems with his fine motor skills, exampled in a sort of shuffling gait and in the fact that he was always dropping things and bumping into people in the street; he couldn't quite meet your gaze either, his eyeballs skewwhiff and swirling about in their sockets, so perhaps he was properly autistic too. But he was totally harmless, but perhaps even a little bit pathetic to boot. Among the social misfits lurking around Speaker's Corner, he introduced me to a guy who used to shuffle around with a sandwich board slung over him, the slogan declaring to the world that 'It's going to get worse', in big black capitals. This was supposed to stimulate passers-by at Speaker's Corner into engaging him in conversation, but when they would ask him exactly what it was that was going to get worse, well then he would simply throw his hands up into the air and declare, 'Why, everything of course!!', and that was the end of that. 'Page Boy' also hung around with a lanky, bearded guy called 'Traveller', who did just that; he wandered on foot from one end of the country to the other and then came back to the KFC at Marble Arch to regale everyone with his tales of adventure and unexpected hospitality. He looked like a bit like a ferret, and I told him this in a moment of glaring autistic candour; he flinched, absorbed the 'slight' and then burst out with an almighty guffaw; 'You're alright Mickey!' he said, slapping me on the back even as he convulsed with laughter.

Another person who'd slipped through the cracks of respectable society and ended up frequenting the KFC and also Speaker's Corner was a little Jewish man called Colin. One day he told me of a hideously deformed monster of a man who lived near the Serpentine in Hyde Park and who was better known to the police as 'The Flashing Green Man'; according to Colin, 'The Flashing Green Man' prowled Hyde Park by night and kidnapped any homeless kids he found hanging out there, dragging them back to his lair to do who knows what with them. Apparently, none of these poor kids was ever seen again. Many were the evenings I thus spent standing at the railings on the corner of Hyde Park nearest Marble Arch, watching the dusk settle and hoping to catch a glimpse of this famed mythical persona. I was quite credulous back then, and to a certain extent I still am; in my experience a great many autistic people have this trait, which I myself consider not entirely unbecoming. I never actually saw 'The Flashing Green Man', but who knows, he might still be out there, lurking down by the Serpentine at dusk, just waiting...

I was at the youth training scheme in Hackney at roughly the same time I was hanging around Hyde Park and the KFC, and 'Page Boy' accompanied me to the premises on a couple of mornings. His vaguely ditzy demeanour didn't go down all that well with the various hardened black kids from the nearby housing estates, nor did his propensity to slobber whenever he got excited endear him to the staff either. I myself was busily being passed from one youth training scheme to the next back in those days, although I ended up staying several years there at the 'Hackney Youth Workforce'. Despite my autism I was so savvy in some respects that the staff had me manning the reception desk during lunch breaks, before quickly bustling me back into the company of all those hardened black kids when they'd finished their sandwiches and their Styrofoam cups of coffee. I made friends with some of the white kids – those hardened black kids didn't quite take to me as a rule – and we spent various sunny afternoons hanging out in nearby parks and sometimes heading off toward the City to see what mischief we might cause. Hackney Youth Workforce was near Old Street, so it wasn't really in Hackney at all – it merely took up the human detritus blowing in from that particular borough. I think the kids liked me because I was weird and wacky and also because I didn't grass when I caught them smoking a joint in the broom closet with one of the female receptionists; I liked this particular receptionist best of all because she used to say, 'He's my favourite!' whenever I arrived at the building, although quite her favourite what I actually was, well of that I wasn't quite sure.

One of the Hackney Youth Workforce staff once took me to the London Hospital for an STD check, after an early and inadvertent sexual 'experience', despite the fact that no one actually laid a finger on me. On a night out in Islington with some friends I'd left it too late to get the train home and ended up staying in the flat belonging to a pair of young gay vicars. I was quite happy on the sofa until one of them marched into the living room at one in the morning, stark naked and 'excited', to promptly inform me that I was to join them in the bedroom forthwith, or else face getting ejected out onto the street. It was cold and dark out and I was 18 and autistic, and so I opted for what I perceived to be the lesser evil of the bedroom, although I refused to let either of them touch me once I got there. I think I spent the better part of an hour huddled in the corner, drawing my knees up to my chest with my arms. They took the hint, leaving me to sit there and endure their rather frenetic little performance; the place veritably stank of amyl nitrate, as I recall. Despite the lack of intimate contact, I became convinced that I had contracted something from them and thus might end up like poor Nicky Crane, and on that basis, I had the aforementioned test at the London Hospital. The test turned up nothing whatsoever, apart from the horrific experience of having one's penis swabbed.

As it turned out, my lack of sexual experience was worlds away from that of my companions at Hackney Youth Workforce, many of whom were busy f***ing for England, with men and women both older and younger than themselves; also with each other; and, so I suspected, even with that pot-smoking female receptionist. My classmate Kevin took great pride in pulling up his West Ham United home shirt and showing me the scratches on his back, administered courtesy of the middle-aged woman he was then seeing, she with a couple of kids under her belt already. One time, some of us wandered into a strip-club/pub just around the corner from the Hackney Youth Workforce building on Old Street, the boys thinking that the sight of all those bits and bobs wobbling around was absolutely hilarious. I wasn't quite sure what to make of it all, but I remember the manager chasing us out into the street, waving his fist, a cigar dangling out the corner of his lips. My mother had always been rather censorious of sexual imagery when I was younger, and I think I occasionally emulated her prudishness by a sort of unwelcome osmosis as I got older. I do remember that as soon as a stray boob or a hint of homosexuality appeared on our TV set she would break the land speed record by diving towards the switches – no remotes back then – and changing the channels before the offending images seared themselves onto my brain, which they mostly still did anyway.

Once, a couple of the kids from Hackney Youth Workforce invited me to a house party in deepest Dalston, but I was too scared to go, turning them down after much mulling and musing. Going to parties seemed a bit too adult and a bit too normal, although I do have a vague memory of popping around to a flat in Hackney one sunny afternoon in the company of several of these classmates for some reason or other. There was no party involved, but I distinctly remember walking along one of those enclosed red-brick walkways you see policemen dashing along in 'gritty' ITV dramas, past shuttered door after shuttered door, all of them with a secondary iron gate bolted over the front. To a boy brought up within the suffocatingly suburban climes of southeast London it was quite the education, especially when first I saw the scorched patch of earth out back that served as a communal garden for the entire block.

When I wasn't hanging around with these disaffected kids from Hackney Youth Workforce, I was riding the buses from Old Street and off into the City, wandering the crowded streets and apologising profusely for my lack of fine motor skills as I bumped into this or that smartly suited person. Every Thursday I took the cream-coloured no.22b bus to the New Oxford Street branch of Forbidden Planet to pick up my weekly comic books. At some point my favourite shop had merged from two branches on Denmark Street (comic books) and sci-fi (St Giles High Street) into one superstore a stone's throw away, on the aforementioned stretch of road. The staff there treated me with a curious mixture of indulgence and disdain, the standard formula of response to autism I'd fast become used to over the years, first discerned when I pitched up at Sight & Sound. One guy at the new Forbidden Planet superstore was so enamoured of me that he used to let me price up the back issues I wanted before I bought them, this of course with reference to a certified comic book pricing guide; when this was discovered he got into all sorts of trouble, and I fretted for a while that I'd be barred from the store, but I wasn't. For a while after that I had the security guards trailing me at a rather indiscreet distance every time I shopped, even though I'd no intent of ever again sticking my own prices on things, with or without the say-so of a staff member.

Anyway, bringing things back to Thursdays, after visiting Forbidden Planet I'd head back towards Hackney Youth Workforce, disembarking somewhere in the City but within walking distance of the premises. Often, I would go and sit somewhere and read my new comics, and also have my lunch at the same time. Sometimes I would eat my sandwiches perched on a wall with seven or eight smartly attired City bankers either side of me. Given where I was – or wasn't – in the career stakes at the time, this was a little like pressing one's nose to the window of a particularly fine restaurant and trying to see what everyone inside was eating on their exceedingly expensive plates. To the endless dismay of NT Me, a place at Hackney Youth Workforce meant that I was about as far away from that sort of life as it was quite possible to be.

'G' is for…

…gross motor skills.

This term basically refers to all of the 'bigger' things you do with your body, starting with crawling about as a little baby, right down to running and jumping around as an adult. Needless to say, when you're saddled with dyspraxia alongside your particular dose of autism, well, these movements can be somewhat compromised, and that was most certainly the case when first I went clubbing. Basically, I hit the dancefloor with all the delicacy of a deranged octopus; no fine motors here, dear, but definitely more of the 'dad dancing' that I mentioned in the previous – and yes, admittedly somewhat similar to this one – chapter.

By now – circa 1993 or so – I was clubbing in London on a semi-regular basis, hanging around with a group of beautiful, misshapen misfits, including a transsexual called Johnny whom we all imaginatively referred to 'Johnny the tranny'; Billy the go-go boy; a drug dealer called LeVent; an Australian boy with a penchant for feather boas called Bobby, who worked in Selfridges and swiped me free samples from his cosmetic counter; Lee, the rotund runaway from Portsmouth; and finally 'Sammi the snakewoman', a willowy blond from Berkshire who frequently stopped traffic with her six foot two statuesque frame. It was Sammi who first suggested that I might 'throw some better shapes' on the dancefloor if I imbibed a few grams of Speed beforehand. She taught me how to gobble the illicit stuff by wrapping it up in some toilet paper and then downing it with a swig of mineral water, holding my nose in case any Speed escaped. It then took about forty-five minutes to kick in, at which point – according to general testimony – shivers run up and down the length your spine, whilst suddenly your gob begins to gabble at approximately 100mph. I could honestly swear that in those few drug-addled hours I actually became your average neurotypical, gassing nonsensically about this and that, certainly when the effects of the drug were at their very peak; NT Me was in the driving seat, and no mistake. I felt considerably more coordinated too, as though Speed were somehow smoothing out the rough edges where those gross motor skills were concerned. The come down from Speed was of course catastrophic; many a Sunday I spent sprawled out in my darkened bedroom, a sour taste on my tongue and a perturbing sense that life was both completely pointless and also utterly futile. I never tried Ecstasy, despite Nicky Crane offering to procure a pill which I might then 'pop' in the relative safety of his Rupert Street flat; I think by then I'd been safely indoctrinated by the media where the adverse effects of 'E' were concerned, whereas Speed never really seemed to get people quite so panicked. That song by The Shamen – 'Ebeneezer Goode' – charted at the time, and this too swayed my decision somewhat, although someone later told me that the lyrics were actually pro-pill popping, but down on the various dealers. All of this was a couple of years before the tragic case of Leah Betts, who died after taking Ecstasy in 1995, but clearly – if my reluctance to partake was anything to go by – already there were sinister stories doing the rounds.

My best friend of this time – and for the next fourteen years or so – was Gary Loveday, a lad several years older than me, and one who also gobbled down prodigious quantities of Speed, but who otherwise lived a quiet, respectful, and decidedly suburban existence down in deepest Surrey. We became friends initially because I wanted someone to share the walk down the Charing Cross Road with, normally at around four in the morning, to where I might pick up the Night Bus in Trafalgar Square. Lee – the rotund runaway from Portsmouth – actually came to live with me for a while at around this time, as did a lanky rough-sleeper from the London Connection called Jordan; my parents were very accommodating, perhaps a touch guilty at failing to give me a decent crack at the academic whip, I never could tell. This offer of accommodation helped Lee inasmuch as it stopped him bunking the train between Portsmouth and London and that also that he had a bolthole from which to flee his stern, military father Mervyn. Like 'Page Boy' before him, Lee was almost certainly lurking somewhere 'on the spectrum', perhaps towards the slightly more forgiving end, passing as a neurotypical rather better – very galling, I must say – than I did. Several years later we pooled our pitiful resources and went on the trip of a lifetime to New York, staying in a hotel on 34th Street that was undergoing renovations, consequently offering cut-price rooms to customers who didn't mind a bit of a noise and a fine film of sawdust over their faces come the morning. We also went to Amsterdam, although my recollections of this particular trip are rather hazy; we rented a cheap 'Airbnb' style apartment, the guy who owned it leaving lots of little complimentary 'gifts' scattered inside bathroom cabinets, under coffee tables and the like; boiled sweets, packets of wet-wipes and condoms, mainly, but no joints. Lee and I lost touch around 1997 and the last I heard of him he'd gone to prison for robbing some guy he was sharing a flat with. I can only think that he suffered some sort of personality disintegration, or maybe a major autistic style meltdown, one that ended up landing him in trouble with the law. It was a shame because he could be a really charming guy when he wanted to. I reasoned – in regard to the loss of this particular friendship – that when you're autistic you tend, I guess by the law of averages, to come across more of the same, the ones who seemed to have slipped through the cracks in society, than if you were nicely neurotypical. Another rather more brutal way to put it might be to say that 'damaged simply attracts damaged'.

During these heady, halcyon days of clubbing, we would often be out until the early hours, trawling the cafes of Soho and occasionally even ending up in some backroom bar that 'decent folk' weren't supposed to know about. Sometimes we went to clubs that didn't even open until six o'clock in the morning; there was one such place on Kingsway, but I couldn't remember for the life of me what it was called. It took a year, all in all, before the party finally turned a little sour. It all started when Sammi's friend Vienna went to prison for dealing Speed. Not long after that, LeVent – then also dealing – got beaten up with baseball bats by a bouncer on whose patch he had blatantly trespassed. It was all terribly 'exciting' and grownup, with me of course quite safely positioned on the periphery of all this drug-fuelled drama. On the plus side, I also met lots of faded/c-list celebrities as they came to our favourite club to do their respective turns; Dannii Minogue saw me in my underwear (twice), and Sandi Shaw let me sip what was left of her Manhattan while we hung about in her dressing room. However, the bubble of 'celebrity' finally burst when I caught Hazell Dean haggling over a minicab fare, soon after her set was over; up the mirrored staircase and out of the club I crept, emerging onto a chilly midnight Charing Cross Road, finding her with hands on hips, a battle-weary expression on her face, after finally having fought the fare down to a mere fiver. 'But you're famous,' I gasped, 'I mean, don't you have a limousine or something?! I mean, you're from the Hit Factory! Stock/Aitken/Waterman, and all that!'

'Mickey,' she said, 'I'm the girl whose records happen to be the left-over album tracks that Kylie recorded first; of course I don't have a limousine.'

During this time, I also had several jobs handing out flyers to people leaving our favourite club and who might then want to move on somewhere else. The shift hours for this little shindig were horrendous, as you didn't even 'clock on' until 1am, and you weren't finished with your flyers until the last sorry dregs had left the club and staggered out into the burgeoning sunlight, at around 4am. Initially I was stationed around Old Compton Street in Soho, hoping to catch people before they decided where they were actually going of an evening. There was a part of me that wanted simply to urge them on home to the comforts of a nice bottle of wine and a good video; as I said, the clubbing craze had somewhat worn off at this point and I was seeking something a little more substantial in my life. I've noticed since then that once you cut clubbing out of the equation it becomes very hard to winkle it back into your life, and probably I haven't set foot in one of those places for over a decade now; some aspects of autism seem to swell and undulate over time, and I think that now I'd probably pass out from sensory overload if I tried to revive my clubbing days. I was twenty or so when I began clubbing and it seemed then that the chance of spending my life suited, booted and working for some flash firm in the City was fading faster even than when I'd at least been in rough geographical proximity, over at Hackney Youth Workforce. There was however one consolation to this particular scenario; thanks to those little dabs of Speed I'd indulged in over the past year, my dyspraxia had indeed smoothed out to such a degree – albeit temporarily – that my gross motor functions were pretty much now perfectly in sync with my mind. This meant that I could at least visualise myself back on that wall in the City, post-lunch and comic books, on my feet and shimmying away behind a row of smartly attired bankers, and not putting a single foot awry as I went; I was there in spirit, at least.

'H' is for…

…hyperresponsiveness.

Now this basically means that normal stimuli – sights & sounds – are sometimes so magnified for an autistic person that they can become almost completely overwhelmed by them. To an outsider, this might manifest almost like a gentle form of hypnosis; trust me, if you're with an autistic person and suddenly they glaze over, chances are they're off somewhere really good and not just simply bored by your company. For me – certainly among my more idyllic sensory sojourns – it was often simply random words, or else words sewn together to form a story, although sometimes a really pleasant sounding word in isolation might leave my senses quite simply spinning; I love the word 'frost', for some reason, and 'crocodile' is quite good too. When this happened, when I felt myself magnetised by some sentence in a novel or something, well, you could liken the effect to that of someone playing a flute in order to mesmerise a cobra up out of a box. Of course, this sensitivity to words dovetailed wonderfully with the fact that I was going to be a writer; perhaps it was the reason why I simply had to be a writer, with all other possible career options kicked to the kerb, NT Me be damned.

On that basis, I began tinkering with a few words of my own; I brought a cheap electric typewriter and crafted a short story that I mailed to a fledgling publishing company based in Wales. I explained to them in the covering letter that I couldn't hope to hold down a regular job, possibly even paraphrasing one of the characters from my favourite novel, Anne Rice's 'The Witching Hour'; '…you know, the only thing I can be is a writer. I'm absolutely unprepared for anything else. When you've lived the kind of life I have, you are good for nothing. Only writing can save you.' It was all very melodramatic, but I was quite caught up in my own oddness back then, and quite happy to capitalise on my bizarre little backstory as best I could.

Anyway, the publishers liked what they saw and they published my short story in their first anthology; in fact they published three of my pieces over the next few years, even though the stories I submitted were somewhat scatological and smutty in nature, the sort of stuff you'd really expect from an overgrown schoolboy as opposed to a budding 'arty' autistic author. In some ways I think that maybe I am still just an overgrown schoolboy; my education derailed at about the age of twelve (I do tend to somewhat labour this point, so please bear with me) and I've been trying to recover it from the wreckage ever since. Still, it was nevertheless quite a heady experience to walk into a Waterstones, pick up a copy of this anthology and to see my name there in print. Whenever I passed a bookstore which stocked the anthology, well, I always made a point of putting a copy amidst the foremost display section, something I later heard a lot of authors tend to do whenever they come across their work in public. My family knew about this short story anthology, but I was too ashamed to show them the actual finished production, concerned it would give them something of a warped window into my rather worrisome nature. I even got a good review for the first story in one of the free London magazines, wherein the critic said that I would '…one day make my mark', but only if I might avoid the frequent and often overbearing use of alliteration; I'm still working on that one. There was an award ceremony for the best short story in that first anthology, held in Aberystwyth, I think at the university. I was so excited that I might win the coveted cash prize that I made the journey there under my own steam, the first time I'd ever been so far from home without company. I didn't win, but some of the people present were quite pleased to meet the lad who'd written that smutty little story that had made them smile so much.

In the wake of this first literary 'success' I enrolled on a creative writing class at Birkbeck, University of London. Nothing much came of it in the way of friendships apart from a reasonably good rapport with the teacher, Paul Hallam; if I wrote anything of note whilst I was there then I no longer have it to hand. It wasn't until several years later that I first encountered the phrase 'pseudointellectual', and I think retrospectively I might apply it to several of my classmates from that first stint at Birkbeck without too much bother. It was all very po-faced; po-faced navel-gazing with the occasional burst of a rather world-weary cynical humour thrown in just for good measure. I stayed friends with Paul Hallam, taking my work around to the flat he rented in Soho, several doors down from where Nicky Crane had once lived; talk between us drifted around various topics besides my propensity for scatological characters, and I remember on one occasion Paul said to me once, 'Everything will happen to you when you're in London, Mickey, the same way everything has happened to me; you'll fall in love, you'll get clobbered…'

'Who would clobber me?!' I gasped.

Paul shrugged. 'You'll get clobbered,' he said again, and

then left it at that.

My literary confidence continued to be so buoyed by all of this that I soon signed on for another course, this time at Morley College in Lambeth, for an A-Level in English language. After all, I'd left school with just that one meagre GCSE in the subject and so I decided that this would herald the beginning of my educational comeback; I would prove beyond any doubt that I wasn't – as several of my teachers and also that wretched doctor had once labelled me – 'educationally backward'. Once I started this class I spent the first few weeks worrying that the teacher – in fact a rather lovely woman – would find my work so disagreeable that she would take me by the wrist and dig her nails into the flesh, often a consequence of displeasing several of my senior school teachers. Pretty soon however, the atmosphere at Morley College enabled me to cultivate a somewhat sunnier attitude, but still the whole socialising thing eluded me; when everyone else went down to the canteen during breaks I would remain in the classroom, hunched up in my big silver puffer jacket, intently leafing through the latest Anne Rice novel. I still couldn't keep up with the way that neurotypicals talked, all of that fluid hand and eye movement, gazing at each other one minute and then drifting away the next; and oh, the physical animation of it all, with one hand going this way and then the head going the other, and so on and so forth. It was a bit like trying to master a particularly puzzling dance-craze, and so for the moment I left them to it. It was much easier to talk to people in a club, where almost everyone was off their face and eye contact tended to involve trying to focus on a pair of bulging, dilated pupils and little else besides.

It was a pity that I didn't make more of an effort with the Morley College class, because they were really nice people and not at all like the bothersome brats who'd made my life so miserable at school; they never punched me and they never spat in my mouth, for one thing. I think that these rather more mature classmates sensed something different about me, but the only time my 'unconventional' lifestyle really leaked into the classroom was when Jordan's face appeared framed in the square of glass set into the door, eyes darting to and fro as he sought me out amongst the studious faces within. It turned out that he'd found himself on the street again and simply couldn't face another stint sleeping in a cardboard box on The Strand. I took him home with me and my mum gave him chicken soup and, as I think I said, he ended up staying for several years, on and off. He was a bit wild and unpredictable but basically harmless, although he had a disconcerting habit of loudly berating the checkout girls at the local Sainsbury's for looking, in his opinion, 'too tarty'. There were lots of homeless people in London back then, in the mid-1990s; the sight of them evaporated in the early 2000s but now – circa 2020 or so – well it's a bit like 1996 all over again. Jordan slept in a put-up bed on my floor, taking great delight in scaring the life out of me by breaking wind in the dead of night, the emission so forceful that it was a little like being awoken by a large explosion.

Several times Jordan tried finding a place of his own, on one occasion the both of us falling in with a guy who helped to rent us a property not far from Baker Street; all was going swimmingly until we spotted him on an edition of BBC1's 'Crimewatch' – apparently he was running a scam 'grooming' vulnerable lads into renting properties and then using the premises as a place to run drugs or something. My mum had to go up to the police station at Baker Street and secure Jordan's freedom when he was unwittingly arrested as an accomplice; I don't know if they ever actually caught the man.

To this day, a vague informal diagnosis of autism/personality disorder/something-or-other hangs over Jordan and he seems quite content to let it stay that way.

Jordan and I would spend night after night playing various Nintendo video games whilst he was living with us. Looking back, well, it seems such a shocking waste of time, but you tend to do these things when you're younger, and it's only when you're older that you realise your days might have been better spent travelling the world or writing a book or something. We went to Edinburgh once, in the autumn of 1996, I think because I wanted to see the various locations where they'd filmed 'Trainspotting'; I also wanted to see if there really were heroin addicts hanging out of every shop doorway on Princes Street. In the end, there wasn't much joy on that front apart from a few dingy, vaguely authentic-looking stairwells, all of them sporting an abundance of discarded syringes scattered over the rain-sodden concrete.

All in all, I finished 1996 in a far better position than I'd started it; I had a slew of published short stories under my belt, and besides that also an A-Level in English language, although the exam was a rather tense and tremulous affair. Buoyed up my newfound academic success, I then signed up for a couple more A-Level courses, both due to begin in the autumn of '96; these would take me right through to the summer of '97, with the possibility of applying for a place at university as a mature student as a result. One of these A-Levels was in philosophy, again at Morley College. I remember the tutor explaining concepts like '...there must be a God or an intentional mastermind behind the human race because the design of the eye is so intricate, so complex, that it simply couldn't have come about by chance, or even to have evolved that way; it must have been nudged in the right direction, so to speak.' It was all very stimulating stuff, and I soon handed in my first piece of coursework with the idea that I might get a pretty decent grade; I'd mentioned in said essay the idea of hyperresponsiveness, and how maybe the eye of an autistic person was yet more intricate still. I had high hopes for that essay. I'd also made a perfectly decent pen pal around this time too, a guy called Bill, who lived in Bradford; like me, Bill was a big 'Star Wars' fan. Bill and I even made tentative plans to meet, with him journeying down to London so that we could watch the special edition of 'The Empire Strikes Back' in the big Odeon in Leicester Square. Life, of course, was busy making other plans; the carefully nurtured dreams of NT Me, that whole slow slog toward 'respectability' – via a return to education – were about to suffer a truly devastating blow...

'I' is for...

...insistence on sameness.

True, this is perhaps not the most lyrically sounding point where neurodiversity is concerned, but then again, I'm not the one having to make these frequently ridiculous diagnostic criteria up. Yes, autistic people are famous – no, make that nigh-on notorious – for their extremely rigid routines, and woe betide anyone who disrupts the diligent running of their daily lives. But I would like to put it out there and suggest, well, who doesn't have a fairly rigid daily routine?!? Do you breathe? Yes? Well congratulations then, you have a rigid routine. Do you eat? Again, well done, you are someone thoroughly set in your ways on multiple levels; do you go to work each day and walk by moving one foot in front of the other?! Well there you go then; it seems that you're a creature of almost consummate habits.

But even an autistic person can become wearied by their routine, and thus given to glancing – on the rare occasion – with some envy at the supposedly fluid lives of their neurotypical neighbours. This may then lead to a longing for that same sort of raucous spontaneity. For example; in the spring of 1997, I was in my early twenties and still stuck living at home, with no proper job and only one GCSE and one recently acquired A-Level to my name. Admittedly I'd had a string of short stories published, but it wasn't like people were banging down my door and waving wonderful publishing opportunities in my face. Therefore, I decided to take matters into my own hands and rupture this rut I found myself in. Now, believe me, if you're autistic you can pretty much expect 'sweet FA' in the way of outside help (I'm talking NHS-style help here) unless you literally present yourself in a semi-suicidal state, perhaps with your wrists slashed and a woe begotten look upon your face. Basically, no one was going to help me and so therefore I had to help myself, to make my own opportunities. And basically, what followed went a bit like this: amongst the regular speakers at the London Connection youth group was a man who came seeking people to volunteer as pen pals for various isolated prisoners within the British penal system. I put my name forward and sent a small letter to an anonymous stranger in a prison somewhere who'd committed a crime I hadn't even considered. It was a feat of astonishing naiveté, and one that only an autistic person might possibly pull off and yet still save face. For all I knew, I might've just struck up a correspondence with a veritable monster, but actually the person who replied was just your run-of-the-mill arsonist/shotgun wielding bank robber; oh, and an alcoholic too, but he didn't disclose that until he had one hand around my throat and the other foraging through my pockets looking for spare change to buy his next bottle of gin. He was, quite literally, what my pen pal Bill would refer to as a '…charming psychopath'. Bill worked in a secure mental health unit in Bradford and our regular late-night phone calls were often interrupted by one of his patients suffering a vague mental health crisis; sometimes Bill would quite suddenly ring off, but on other occasions he might leave the receiver dangling and myself on the other end listening attentively for the echoed sounds of some sort of schizoid showdown. Of course, by the time Bill had administered the diagnosis of 'charming psychopath' to my new pen pal it was much, much too late to do anything about it…

I didn't know it at the time, but this guy in prison that I was corresponding with – Robbie – would actually end up providing me with my first chance at moving out of home and establishing a vaguely independent life for myself. Robbie was due for release within the next few months of our initial correspondence, and he made a big thing in his letters about setting up a new life for himself in Oxford. He didn't want to embark on this great adventure alone and so he basically talked me into setting up a new life for myself alongside him. To be perfectly honest it sounded great, full of promise and sunshine – it was a swelteringly hot spring – and a world away from the increasingly samey streets of London. Because I'd missed so much school, I was entirely unawares of Oxford's venerable history as a bastion of academic achievements, but once I found out, well then the idea of living there really began to snowball. I'd only actually been to Oxford once before, to see my friend Victor Bullock being ordained as a vicar; I remember being encouraged to turn around at the end of the service and say 'Peace be with you' to the people in the pew behind, even though it seemed to be one of those standard neurotypical exercises in complete and utter insincerity. It felt like when people say, 'Oh we must meet up!' and then they never bother to get in contact; or maybe that only happens to me lots, because I'm often so autistically insufferable. Anyway, Victor was a friend of the groping gay vicars from Islington, although in that particular instance he'd poured Biblically righteous scorn on their dubious activities. I didn't get on terribly well with many of Victor's other friends, though; when I went to stay with him in Teddington, well, his landlord took one look at me and then said to Victor, 'I really wish you wouldn't bring rent back to the house, dear.'

Robbie began writing to me fairly regularly. After a while he also began enclosing cassette tapes along with his letters, apparently as a random afterthought, although it soon settled into a fairly regular pattern. These tapes often contained hours and hours' worth of one-sided conversation, alongside reminiscences of his childhood in Redcar, sometimes with other prisoners popping into his cell to share their own dismal stories. Robbie also started calling my home as well, regular as clockwork at 6pm every evening and eventually on weekends as well; it was like a proper adventure, this whole business of corresponding with a crook. Occasionally he couldn't call, because of a riot or some other unsavoury disturbance, upon which I tried not to let my propensity for an 'insistence on sameness' to shine through; the fact that I would be sat by the phone for anything up to an hour, chewing my fingernails and wringing my hands was the only outward sign that things weren't going quite as clockwork as planned.

As well as hailing from Redcar, Robbie was also about ten years older than me, and intensely practical. He didn't initially twig that I was autistic, basically because our contact was at this stage purely epistolary; also, my autistic penchant for showy penmanship allowed me to acquit myself quite admirably on paper, painting a pretty dazzling but somewhat deluded self-portrait in the process; the reality – for the both of us, I fear – was quite different when finally we met up in the flesh.

I went to Oxford by myself to suss the place out, several weeks ahead of Robbie's release date. I took the Oxford Tube coach service from near Victoria Station, a trip I would end up making fairly regularly, when it transpired that I didn't like the rotund, pawing gay vicars that Robbie had arranged for me to stay with. Once

Robbie was actually released, well then I ended up 'roughing it' in the occasional hotel, but initially I was still mainly based at home; whether they were young or fat, I'd had a resoundingly bad time where gay clergy and their occasionally disturbing predilections were concerned. However, I most certainly liked what I saw of Oxford on that solo reconnoitre. There were some half-decent pubs and lots of studious looking people striding along the streets, clutching their books to their chests and looking very serious and troubled; they were thinking big thoughts, quite possibly. One could go punting on the Thames in Oxford or wander for hours down seemingly endless stretches of venerable, cobbled lanes, wherein I discovered countless 'olde worlde' shops cluttered full of marvellous second-hand books and the like.

When first he was released from prison, Robbie went to live in a bail hostel on the Abingdon Road. The Abingdon Road was one of the main arteries in and out of Oxford, close enough for convenience to the historic city centre but far enough away for one to bear witness to the starkly contrasting reality of council houses and old men slumped on park benches, swigging booze from bottles wrapped in brown paper bags. The red-brick bail hostel had a strict curfew and all the residents were required to be indoors every evening by 10pm; this was late June, so that meant roughly sunset. As a resident, Robbie was required to do various chores and also various 'rehabilitation' workshops, these to be attended on an almost daily basis. I therefore ended up having ample time on my hands to explore the surrounding Hinksey Park area. All of this gave me independence of a sort, and certainly the break from 'insistence on sameness' that I'd been seeking; you'd be amazed, really, at how the average autistic person rises to a challenge, even one that was, on reflection, rather a risqué one. The fact that the whole thing would end up being so very ruinous to NT Me's carefully nurtured plans of respectability seemed – back then, certainly – little more than a vaguely troubling shimmer on an otherwise balmy horizon. What my parents thought of the whole thing I couldn't imagine – autistics empathise better with animals, on the whole – but I remember on that fateful morning when first I set out for Oxford that my mother wept as she saw me off at the front door. Giving my mother her due, it must be said – reiterated, even – that autistic people aren't famed for their good judgement; we're just simply too kind and trusting, tending to see the best in everyone, which means that the sourness of everyday life often comes to us as something of a rude slap about the face.

The owners of the various hotels that I stayed in on the Abingdon Road soon cottoned on to the fact that I was consorting with someone from the bail hostel. Now, with hindsight, I can sympathise with them; it can't have done their trade much good to have their businesses located in the immediate vicinity to such a veritable '…hive of scum and villainy', to paraphrase 'Obi-Wan Kenobi', via my pen pal Bill. Eventually, most of these hotels actually banned me – you get used to this sort of dismissive refusal when you're on 'the spectrum' – but by then Robbie had almost served his time in the bail hostel anyway, and was due to be released into the world at large on a more formal basis. Before that happened, various minor dramas of one sort or another unfolded at the bail hostel; one of the residents tried to kill himself, found with wrists slashed and passed out down a dusty pathway leading into the fields near Christ Church college; on another occasion Robbie himself got drunk on some bootleg booze and broke his curfew, which was pretty much a cardinal sin where the hostel staff were concerned. That was the time when he ended up with one hand around my throat and the other busily rifling my pockets for any loose change, the better to buy yet more booze; to make matters worse, he then tore his top off in the middle of the street and started wailing on about what a terrible life he'd had. I recall a passing biker offering me an escape route on his backseat, but foolishly I elected to remain and help the person with whom I'd thrown in my sorry lot. Because Robbie had actually broken his bail conditions on that particular evening, the police were duly called, by which time he'd taken refuge in my latest hotel; cue a police helicopter scouring the length of the Abingdon Road, and me sequestered in the room's lone closet, mumbling almost incoherently that the whole thing – the entire endeavour, even – was simply one enormous mistake, a giant lapse of admittedly dubious autistic judgement.

As a result of his drunken misdemeanour, Robbie was given a strict dressing down – as was I – by his probation officer; the regular fortnightly visits to her office were always a delight in utter dismalness. He was put on some sort of medication that made him violently sick if he drank any alcohol, forced to stand there and swallow the pill each morning with one of the hostel staff observing. This, I found, was the less glamourous, rather more pitiful side of crime that one rarely bears witness to in TV dramas and the like; the effect on myself as a witness was almost as stupefying as it was on Robbie himself.

All of this occurred during the extremely long, hot summer of 1997, when Tony Blair became prime minister and when Princess Diana met her 'accidental' death in that tunnel in Paris; the latter certainly was one of those 'where were you when it happened?!?' moments. I was actually at home in bed at the time, awoken by a phone call from a pub acquaintance called 'Fat Carl'; as a family we went downstairs and turned on the news to see if what I'd been told was actually true. This was in the early hours of the morning and as yet Princess Diana hadn't actually died, but news of the 'accident' was still shocking enough that I had a panic attack on the spot, almost asphyxiating because no one could find me a brown paper bag to breathe into. Robbie was visiting his family in Redcar when it happened, having been given permission by the hostel; I remember calling him that Sunday morning – I'm sure it was a Sunday – and hearing his mum in the background gasping, 'My god, it's true!' as she turned on the TV. About a week later, Robbie and I watched the huge state funeral, lolled on the bed in the humid little room he occupied in the bail hostel, directly overlooking the Abingdon Road. The potency of the summer heat was by then beginning to wane somewhat, and our strolls through Hinksey Park and beyond – mainly to the General Elliot pub in nearby Hinksey Village – were becoming few and far between. I was surviving on cash bundles courtesy of my mother and these too were thinning somewhat both in their frequency and also in their generosity. I applied for a job in an antique shop on the high street, almost securing the position until Robbie, himself something of a dubious expert, waded in and tried to impress the owner with his knowledge of markers and the like, attempting to fob him off with a cheap heart-shaped silver casket that he said was actually a '...vintage cigarette case belonging to one of the Russian Tsars'; we were told in no uncertain terms never to return. Despite this curt dismissal, Robbie still clung to the idea that he was one of the great overlooked antiques dealers of the country, and would refer to any little find in a bric-a-brac shop as 'treasure'; I would smile on benignly and reflect that my collection of 70s 'Batman' comics were probably worth more than the latest bit of tat that he'd just handled.

*

Robbie and I eventually settled on Bournemouth once he'd finished with the bail hostel in Oxford. At this point he was moving out of the armed robbery business and into the making of homemade greetings cards, decoupage designs that looked quite charming until the cheap glue dried up and the various 3D bits peeled off. Also, he was still claiming to have been something of an antiques dealer in his previous life – 'Lovejoy', his mother called him – but he looked more like Jimmy Nail than Ian McShane, with his wonky nose and his missing front teeth – lost in a prison brawl – leaving a lower jaw that extended forward in that alarming way one often finds with pensioners sans their 'falsies'. I had an old friend called Gerry who wore false teeth, and the first time I saw him without them I nearly fainted from shock, that is before the usual autistic candour kicked in; 'Someone's taken the scaffolding out of your face!' I gasped. Regarding prison brawls, well, it was from Robbie that I learnt lots of 'useful' titbits on defending myself if ever I were to wind up behind bars, including the classic 'battery in the sock' routine, as well as the use of sugar in boiling water as a permanent way of defacing any would-be assailants; this 'sage' advice was usually proffered over a Coca-Cola and a bag of Walkers Worcester sauce crisps, at the Head of the River pub, just shy of Oxford's Folly Bridge. I didn't really like to tell Robbie that I already knew about a hundred different ways to cosh someone, courtesy of 'Prisoner: Cell Block H', highly recommended by none other than Nicky Crane, who'd done a few stints inside himself.

After Robbie was released from the bail hostel, we took our belongings down to Bournemouth and rented an attic flat in a leafy side street near the idyllic sounding Horseshoe Common. Bournemouth had been beautiful when we'd visited during the summer – special leave from the hostel duly obtained – even if I'd had my very first panic attack in a B & B near the seafront when I'd found out that 'Robbie' and 'alcohol' went together like 'crack' and 'addict'. However, Bournemouth in winter was a different tale altogether, and this seasonal discrepancy is – apparently – a warning of woe that resounds throughout coastal towns the length and breadth of the country, come the autumn chill; what is splashy and exciting in summer is dismal and dank when in winter. To compound the problem, we didn't know anyone in Bournemouth and there precious little money to spend and thus nowhere really to go; the dusty comic shop about a mile from the flat became one of my only idylls, wherein I could make a 22-page issue of 'Deadpool' last for hours. Whenever Robbie got his benefits cheque he immediately trotted off to the local ASDA and blew it all on booze, on one occasion bringing home a big cardboard container of wine with a tap in the side. He then proceeded to spend the entire day slowly drinking it, lying directly underneath and manipulating the tap with his outstretched hand; anticipating the waspish witticisms that would undoubtedly soon spew forth from his mouth, I attempted downing some of the stuff myself. Unfortunately, autism and alcohol tend not to mix, and I ended up pouring most of my share down the toilet. This was all well and good until he caught me committing this sacrilege, attempting to throttle the life out of me, right there as I knelt on the bathroom floor with the empty glass in my hand; I feigned losing consciousness so that he would slacken his grip and then I laid there for several hours waiting for him to drunkenly pass out, back in the living room. On another occasion when 'under the influence', well, then he locked me in the windowless kitchen without benefit of light – the switch was on the wall outside – before informing me that he was thinking of reigniting his career as an arsonist, with torching the flat a possible first return foray; oh, those happy minutes as I sat there with my arms wrapped around my legs, waiting to pass out from smoke inhalation.

Matters weren't helped by the fact that his best friend in prison – still there at this point – was having an affair with one of the female warders with whom Robbie was still quite well acquainted. This woman made frequent visits to Bournemouth to relay news between Robbie and his best friend, at least until the whole sorry tale was exposed by The News of the World. I myself was a mere distant appendage to the dalliances and so my name was mercifully kept out of the papers, but it was a sobering reminder of the sort of people I'd thrown my lot in with. I still harbour vague memories of a clandestine meeting at a house somewhere in Banbury where we had to run inside for fear of being spotted by waiting paparazzi. It was all very melodramatic, and certainly I was too young and too autistic to realise that I might actually end up being implicated in the misdemeanours of this bunch of ne'er-do-wells. Eventually, I was able to reassure myself of a lucky escape by showing to horrified friends and family the various newspaper cuttings detailing the nefarious exploits of Robbie and his cohorts; collective sighs of relief and prayers thanking the almighty for my safe deliverance were duly uttered by all and sundry.

In the end, I became so bored in Bournemouth that even the prospect of getting up in the morning filled me with fear; I spent entire days huddled beneath the duvet, counting off the moments until the Christmas invite extended by my parents took effect. It was funny, but after all that fervour of wanting to break away and be like everyone else – something NT Me still strongly applauded – my autistic insistence on sameness was now insisting that I return home to my former routines, abandoning this foolish venture and filing it away as a colourful anecdote to stimulate conversations in the years to come. The fact of Robbie drunkenly throwing up all over my parents' house on New Year's Day 1998 convinced me that the liaison really wasn't going anywhere, but it was left to my dad to articulate it to Robbie in words that he could understand, such was the strength of his hangover. And so, Robbie went back to Bournemouth and I stayed where I was, pulled back into place by that invisible thread of autistic elastic sameness. He and I kept in touch for a few months afterwards and I went down to visit several times, but it was clear by then that we had nothing in common and that the whole thing had been one giant judgement of error, probably on both our parts. I never officially 'came out' to him as autistic, although it was pretty obvious that I could be as weird as he was, in my own non-alcoholic, non-gun wielding way; he was kind enough to write me a card, several weeks after the rift, where he said of me that '...you're not a person – you're an experience'. Well, I thought to myself, that's one way of detailing a dalliance with the neurodiverse.

'J' is for...

…joint attention.

Now, this doesn't refer to the notion of keeping your limbs supple because, being autistic, one often finds oneself socially isolated and thus spending long periods indoors. No, this form of joint attention refers to encouraging others to take an interest in the very things that you yourself find so utterly absorbing. After the car-crash of my experience with Robbie, and having returned to the proverbial family nest, my penchant – indeed the penchant of a great many autistics – for obsessing over various subjects returned with a vengeance. Perhaps for me this was simply a way of soothing the social blow of moving back home after making that first all-important break, but either way, with time on my hands I soon found myself at the mercy of several all-new, all-different and certainly all-consuming obsessions. The only difference was that now I had absolutely no one with whom to share them, therefore rather jarring the whole notion of my joint attention.

Firstly, I discovered the French poet Arthur Rimbaud,

this during the spring/summer of 1998, when my psyche was still so bruised by the experiences in Oxford and Bournemouth that I wondered momentarily whether or not I would ever really be me again; 'I is somebody else' indeed. I was more taken with Rimbaud's rather weird and wonderful life as opposed to poring over his poetry, most of which I found rather impenetrable; I've tried reading some several times since and I still can't understand it, but maybe I'm just being waylaid by the vast commentary of awe which percolates around it. Rather more than the poetry I liked the person, that he was taciturn and often appeared antisocial, and that he had a pronounced and unusual gait; and of course, that peculiar penchant for viewing vowels as colours.

I brought as many books on Rimbaud as I could manage; and then, via the enthusing of my joint attention, I even persuaded someone to take me to Rimbaud's hometown of Charleville, in the Ardennes in Northern France. I posed for a picture with the Rimbaud bust in the town square and I spent hours walking around the Rimbaud Museum, frustrated that I couldn't read the tags on the exhibits because they were in French and I hadn't been in school long enough to master even the basics. It was far more than a hobby, however; really it was the aforementioned all-consuming passion, the sort so very particular to the neurodiverse. I doubt I could do justice in trying to explain the mania that envelopes one at such times, a failing which is perhaps a blow to the very notion of joint attention; I'm perhaps not selling it enough, in other words. But really, you don't need me to tell you how wonderful Rimbaud is; go and look him up for yourself, if you don't believe me.

I also visited Berlin on the same trip that encompassed Charleville, but found the former utterly underwhelming; no breathtaking landmarks, apparently because they'd all been bombed to bits during the Second World War; again, I hadn't been in school long enough to learn anything tangible about the Second World War apart from the fact that it was all started by someone called Hitler. The Rimbaud pilgrimage and the Berlin visit took place against the regular weekly backdrop of volunteering at the Drury Lane branch of Oxfam, a stone's throw from the famous theatre. Each and every day I worked the till, passing the time in-between customers by poring over the various minutiae of Rimbaud's life. Occasionally I would rifle the donations ahead of distributing them to the shelves, in case I stumbled upon something I felt that I deserved more than some early theatregoer doing a bit of last-minute charity shopping. I socialised occasionally with some of the other volunteers but as always it was like I was communicating through a pane of glass, and I never saw or heard from any of them ever again.

Eventually, I became so enamoured of Rimbaud that I began to write stories and essays about him in my spare time; Patti Smith and Bob Dylan – also enthusiasts – had nothing on me once I really got going. This dovetailed with the fallout from Robbie, helping to reignite the academic achievement of getting that English language A-Level. On that basis I was encouraged to see if I could perhaps win a place at university as a mature student, even though I'd failed to finish that philosophy A-Level at Morley College. I was egged on in this regard by a dear friend called John Geach, someone who'd spun out of the same circle of friends that included Victor the vicar; John Geach put some clerical work my way as part of the consultancy firm he ran. He had a disarming tendency to call me 'little horror' as he peered at me over the tops of his wire-framed glasses. But he was immensely knowledgeable, working over my university application forms with aplomb and also providing a much-needed character reference. I think I took Robbie to meet him at his Croydon flat at some point, during which visit Robbie tried to win him over by naming several of the flat's furnishings as 'lost treasures', a confidence trick John Geach dismissed as '…utter rot' right there on the spot.

Anyway, I applied for the English Literature degree course at London South Bank University, and on the strength of a particularly powerful rant about Rimbaud's reputation – not to mention the publication of my several short stories – I was offered a place to start in September 1998. I hurriedly handed in my voluntary notice at the Drury Lane Oxfam with almost immediate effect; as I said, I hadn't gone down too well with several of the staff there as it was, with one of them even going so far as to accuse me of not lifting up the toilet seat before I took a pee; I'm still working on a witty comeback for that one.

Initially I was somewhat apprehensive regarding this application to enter the hallowed halls of higher education. In the main I was worried that it might turn out to be a rerun of school, but NT Me for one was positively ecstatic at the move; better late than never after all, and I was only in my early twenties at the time. I never realised back then that I'd enjoy the experience of higher education so much that I'd never really leave; perhaps even then I harboured secret notions of making it all the way to the esteemed rank of 'professor'; I'm still working on that one, at present.

The London South Bank campus was located in and around the Elephant & Castle area, several buildings spread over a small distance this way and that, with the little shopping centre sat right at the centre, like a convenient starting point (the railway station is situated directly above it). Most people really don't rate the Elephant & Castle shopping centre at all, but to this day I still think it's sort of cosy. As I had to pass through it heading to and from the station on a daily basis, I became used to the little shops selling secondhand textbooks and cut-price greetings cards; my neurodiverse neurons will undulate violently if ever they finally decide to tear the place down. I used to spend ages in the WHSmiths reading the various magazines, sometimes to the consternation of the manager, who would often come and pluck whatever I was perusing out from my hands before hurriedly ushering me towards the exit. The adjacent tower block in which I had most of my lessons for that first year has long since vanished, and on the site now stands a soaring skyscraper/apartment complex with big glass windows, allowing you to see all the doings of the various occupants when you're standing on the nearby elevated station platform.

I got on well with the other people on the English Literature degree course, although they were for the most part somewhat younger than me. They were also – as far as I could guess – fairly neurotypical. I think it was obvious to them there was something a little uncanny/weird about me, and as a result the person I ended up hitting it off best with was the vaguely spotty boy who seemed the least likely to get a girl; beggars couldn't be choosers where either of us were concerned, I supposed, which took me back to 'Page Boy' a bit. But this boy – Paul – nevertheless possessed a sort of sideways access to the orbit of the other, more popular lads, lads like Luke Hammond, who walked around literally dripping in busty blondes. Via spotty Paul, I was able to work my way up the daunting social ladder of the neurotypical undergraduate, impressing them with my general knowledge playing the pub quiz machines and stuff like that; it's amazing what you can pick up when you're locked up in the house for years on end with only an incomplete set of 'The Joy of Knowledge' as your companion. However, whilst I was a whizz when it came to answering questions concerning contemporary popular culture, it soon became clear that I wasn't quite cut out for a life of academia, or at least not a life of academia with an English Literature slant. The fact that one of the poetry tutors had wrinkled her nose in distaste when I'd proudly presented her with one of my Rimbaud books probably didn't help. Mainly, I was struggling to complete the various incumbent essays, and it was on that basis that things really began to unravel. I enlisted a friend from a fellow course to help me write an arduous piece about something or other that I now forget entirely; this lad called Dave was studying criminology, and in the mess of writing multiple papers he managed to plagiarise my piece to the point where I was summarily booted off the English Literature degree; the more things change, the more they stay the same. For a few brief days a sort of social and professional apocalypse loomed, but in true neurodiverse fashion I rose to the challenge accordingly, determined that I would still get my due where the education system was concerned. I set about pointing out to my disappointed tutors the quality of my previous essays on Rimbaud and on that basis one of the administrators had a quiet word with one of the sociology tutors, given that this was the direction that some of said essays were swinging. As a result, I began my BSc sociology in the autumn of 1999. This time around I was based mainly in the big, rather grand-looking Borough Road building, and occasionally in the London Road building, which had the sort of layout – long main hall with side corridors flanking, repeated on upper levels – that one normally associates with a prison. I never really saw Paul or Luke Hammond or any of the other students from the English Literature degree again, except once when exiting the Borough Road building with my new friends; Luke Hammond, Paul and various others were heading towards us from the opposite direction, in a vaguely boisterous 'lads-in-a-group' style swagger. They didn't acknowledge me but as they drifted on by, I heard Luke Hammond whisper to Paul, 'Did you say hello to him?', with the answer coming in the form of a resounding negative.

1999 saw the first 'Star Wars' movie hit the big screen for several decades, and what a damned disappointment that turned out to be. I won't go into too much detail about how we queued for ten straight hours outside the big Odeon in Leicester Square to be among the first to buy tickets, or the fact that we – Bill, Dave and I – endured seeing it twice on the first day of release because of the hype; now there's joint attention for you. The summer of 1999 also saw me stricken down with a series of particularly bad panic attacks, perhaps brought about by the momentary uncertainties surrounding my newfound academic career. Now, the point to a panic attack is that you think you're going to suffocate/have a heart attack/die; after the sixth or seventh panic attack, when none of these things has happened, well then the panic attacks begin to subside. At least, that's how it went with me. They were still quite terrifying at the time, though, and there was a period of several days when I refused to leave the house entirely, just in case I succumbed to the faux suffocation in public. On one occasion I even had myself driven to the A & E of a busy London hospital, convinced that I was actually going to have a heart attack; I was fast-tracked to the front of the queue, before finding rather embarrassingly that my breathing was in fact returning to normal and that the all-consuming panic had yet again subsided. Another time I had a panic attack on a Night Bus, whilst making the arduous journey home from Trafalgar Square. I was sat upstairs all by myself – it was a weekday evening – and quite how I lasted without flinging myself off the vehicle and seeking help within the murky streets of South London I'll never know.

I took to sociology rather well; so well in fact that I'm still doing it to this day, albeit eventually at the level of a PhD. This was a feat that I couldn't possibly have fathomed back in the autumn of 1999, when I picked up my pencils and pens and moved myself over to London

South Bank's sociology department, based mainly in the aforementioned Borough Road building. For the most part I flourished, although when it came to the data analysis module, I discovered that the festering scab of failed maths lessons was still painfully apparent. One time I ended up sat in the dean's office during the data analysis exam and basically sobbing my heart out. I think I had to repeat the entire module as a result of flubbing that exam. I passed in the end though, mainly by training my neurodiverse nature to hone in on something other than Rimbaud and comics books, cramming as much as possible where qualitative and quantitative data methods were concerned; it can be done, proving that one isn't entirely at the mercy of one's autistic whims after all. Perhaps you might even consider it a somewhat novel demonstration of joint attention, whereby the social aspirations of NT Me won out for the first time in an age, cajoling me into absorbing a subject that the world considered infinitely more practical than either the aforementioned Rimbaud or comic books.

In the end I still had to repeat an entire year of my undergrad degree before I was able to graduate; as a result I was forced to sit there and look on with simmering resentment as my friends – Dave, Richard, Robyn and Maggie in particular – all graduated as scheduled. I watched as they mutually tossed their mortar boards into the air and wondered who might be around to witness the fact when it was my turn. As a result of the data analysis debacle, my last year at London South Bank was a somewhat lonely, isolated affair, even by autistic standards; I was tagged onto the classes of various incoming students or else wrenched back to sit in on seminars I'd previously completed. In my various apprehensions I ended up missing an essay deadline for a World War II holocaust module and had to plead my genuine innocence to the rather hard-nosed tutor; I was allowed to submit the essay, albeit within the space of forty-eight hours. I passed that module with flying colours but nevertheless the whole repeat year had a vaguely 'flying by the seat of my pants' feel to it. When finally I graduated, I was still barely on first name terms with most of my classmates, but at least I got to shake hands with Sir Trevor McDonald as I strode across the stage at Southwark Cathedral for the ceremony. Having said that, the whole notion of the ceremony itself was so surreal – to someone who'd left school aged twelve – that I wasn't quite sure afterwards whether or not I'd actually imagined the whole thing.

'K' is for…

…Kennedy, Anna.

Now an OBE, Anna Kennedy's kids are both autistic, and her struggle to find a decent education for them eventually led her remortgaging her house and then opening several schools specifically catering for children on 'the spectrum'. She now campaigns tirelessly to raise awareness of autism through a variety of different mediums, especially so on Twitter. These noble interventions were a little too late to help me and others of previous generations – 'Their arses are in butter, these millennial aspies', a weary old savant once said to me – but her efforts still meant that there was somewhere for me to seek guidance when first I sought out the company of others like myself. To this end I contacted the Anna Kennedy website and from there was duly directed into attending my first ever autism social event, in the upstairs room of a little pub around the back of Carnaby Street. This gathering was populated by people from all sides of 'the spectrum', and a fair few perhaps even from a bit beyond that. I shared a soda with the odd savant or two, and also crossed paths with those poor souls so blighted by autism that they merely sat in the corner mumbling, and with their eyes rolling, furtively glancing this way and that; '…there but for the grace of God…' I thought, several times. I didn't really strike up a friendship with any of the people that I met – unless you count future Facebook acquaintances – but it all helped me to see with my own eyes that I wasn't the only person in the world whose brain was wired a little differently.

Attending a few more gatherings in the following months produced slightly more mixed results; I was in a pub in the City of London on one occasion when several of the younger members of the group decided to partake in a food fight, this despite the fact that we were surrounded on all sides by swaggering City boys and calculating career women. As I sat there with spiced chicken wings flying to and fro over the top of my head, I thought, '…they can't help it, they just have difficulties conforming to social expectations…', but the looks we were getting from those other patrons were positively filthy; never had I felt quite so distant from NT Me's vision of myself as a suited, booted City of London slicker. I skulked out of the back entrance with a cartoon raincloud of shame hanging over my head, vowing never to meet up with that particular group ever again. However, of them all, I was proud to stay in contact with a young lad called Josh, who worked full-time in a vague admin position at University College London. I was a bit jealous of Josh because he'd secured full-time employment and to some extent seemed to be 'living the neurotypical dream', although how much he really was assimilated into that world I was never entirely sure. As far as outward appearances were concerned, I felt that I 'passed' a little better than he did, but to be brutally honest that discrepancy only served to rub me up the wrong way even more. 'Passing' can be a potentially spiky subject where autistic people are concerned, but it's a topic they're at least willing to tackle without resorting to the sorts of histrionics that often accompany discussions regarding race, gender, or sexuality. 'Passing' basically means whether or not you, as an autistic person, can or indeed are in fact willing to 'mask' (the term often trends on Twitter) in order to try and pass for 'normal'/neurotypical. Sometimes I can pass pretty well, and it's certainly easier if the person I'm with knows that I'm autistic because then if I 'lapse' it doesn't matter so much; trying to 'pass' against someone who doesn't know I have autism is of course a lot trickier, especially if you happen to have a little 'slip' or 'behaviour'.

Of course, many people – and I'm sure Anna Kennedy would count herself among them – would argue that one shouldn't have to try and 'pass' at all, that society should simply accept us as we are. That's a nice idea, but the real world is raw and brutal and in my experience it doesn't really work that way. I've learnt the hard way that whilst people can be tolerant, this is often only up to a point, and not particularly tolerant at all where 'unusual' behaviours are concerned, especially when said 'unusual' behaviours are being exhibited by adults. But I digress (perhaps I should plaster this little rant under 'P'). The point is, I considered that I 'passed' better than Josh, so it narked me that he was doing so well on the job scene, but he was also a 'Doctor Who' fan, so that at least served to level the playing field a little. I was at a signing in Forbidden Planet once when Josh spotted me across the crowded queue, wandering over to talk with me and my friend Neil. It was quite clear – to me at least – which one of us was the more 'obvious', but when eyebrows were raised at poor Josh and the odd snigger was heard, well then I turned and glared at the naysayers nevertheless; jealous of Josh I surely was, but however we look or sound, we neurodiverse really do need to stick together.

*

Further contact with Anna Kennedy's website also enabled me – via a friendly suggestion – to find a way of leaving home for a second time. On this occasion I was able to share a flat with my South Bank friend Dave, who lived in Islington. The end of his street was a favoured spot for fly-tippers and there was a pretty scary looking council estate just beyond that, but I was buoyed up by the fact that Tony Blair lived just around the corner, and also because Islington had a reputation for being 'terribly trendy', even if our street didn't particularly seem as such. On opening the front door of the flat, a little hallway led off to the living room on the right, with the 'bright and breezy' kitchen beyond that; on the left side of the hallway sat a windowless bathroom and straight ahead of that the bedroom, with just enough space therein to squeeze in two singles. We shared the back garden with the occupants of the house above, but they rarely made any demands on the space and as a result we pretty much had free rein to do what we wanted with it. During the course of a hot summer we hosted several barbecues among some of our university friends, but I wasn't much of a fan of these little soirees because I liked my home space to be pretty much private. Dave's parents visited fairly frequently as well – they lived in a council flat in deepest Tottenham – as did his sister, but I didn't get on particularly well with her. She worked a beauty counter in Harvey Nichols and seemed as vague and shallow as the patter she passed off to her potential customers, although I suspect it was secretly more the fact that I envied her natural, easy/neurotypical way with people.

Dave wasn't an alcoholic like Robbie, but it turned out that he did have other substance abuse issues which would end up having a rather insidious impact on my life; a year or so after I moved in, he got himself addicted to crack cocaine. This began with him disappearing from the flat for weeks, if not months on end, to the point where I thought I would end up being the sole occupant and that his pending sociology degree would remain unfinished. When finally he did turn up early one morning – and in a fairly frantic state – he said that he'd been '…kidnapped' by crack dealers and that any money I could give him would be much appreciated; I told him that I was skint and then rolled over and went back to sleep. He soon tottled off and I don't think I saw him after that for about a fortnight. Several weeks later – early September – he made the mistake of bringing a couple of his fellow junkies back to the flat when he thought I wasn't going to be around. Now, many autistic people are by nature shy and retiring sorts, and I can certainly squeeze myself into these respective boxes safely on any given day, but when I found myself confronted with these two nervous, chattering creatures with their dirty fingernails and their wild eyes, well then something in me just snapped; for maybe five minutes it was NT Me firmly in the driving seat. I told them in no uncertain terms to get the hell out of my flat, even threatening to set Anna Kennedy on them if they didn't comply with my command immediately. I don't think they had much idea who Anna Kennedy actually was, but when I tossed in the words '…OBE' this, and '…president of…' that, well, I think that they were suitably impressed/chastened, scarpering out the door and up those steep stone steps as fast as their tatty Converse trainers could take them. Dave went with them and made no apologies for the fact.

That evening I packed up everything I could – including the two cats, Wolvie and Tiggy – and I took them back to my parental home; for a second time I'd been ousted out of my independence on account of my own poor judgement meeting and greeting the flawed character of the person I'd chosen to throw my lot in with. This time round it was even more mortifying because I'd totalled up the impressive term of almost eighteen months living at the Islington flat, whereas the stint at Oxford and

Bournemouth was probably just a little over eight months all in all, give or take the hospitality of a couple of groping gay vicars. A few days after I'd left the Islington flat, Dave pitched up at my parents' house in a dreadful state; dirty, unwashed and half-crazy with what he'd done. In fact, so convinced was he that the drug dealers were following him that he'd crawled along our road on his hands and knees, dodging between cars before making a sudden mad dash toward our front door. My dad duly accompanied him back to Islington, dressed in his best grey pinstripe suit and carrying a briefcase full of absolutely nothing whatsoever. He found my former flat in a terribly distressed state, completely overrun by this marauding gang of crack addicts, with empty pizza boxes and dubious bits of burnt tinfoil scattered about all over the place. He passed himself off as an indignant council worker come to evict them, ahead of an imminent police raid; crazy as it sounds, this little stunt actually worked. Dave cleaned up his act and reclaimed his flat, and we're still friends to this day. I, Dave and Gary Loveday went on to form a fairly decently triumvirate, pubbing and clubbing and taking occasional trips to Blackpool, Bournemouth and occasionally even beyond; Rome was a particular highlight. This set-up – despite Dave's inclusion – helped me survive the initial shock of finding one's home invaded by crack addicts, before then being forced to flee back to my parents. You see, autistic people can be both very forgiving and yet sometimes quite happily hold a grudge for the rest of their lives; it all depends how you slighted them in the first place, and therefore the key word here is 'intent'; Dave hadn't intentionally become a crack addict, rather it was a weakness in his character, not a move made in a moment of calculated spite. Therefore, it followed that he didn't deliberately drag those two crackheads back to the flat purely to scupper my attempts at setting up an independent life, even though it all basically boiled down to the fact that I then couldn't risk hanging around and thus possibly ending up as a fresh convert to the stuff myself.

I remember warming to this more balanced view of things by contacting the Anna Kennedy website and explaining my predicament to them. I'd always thought that a neurotypical person never really understands the strange and rather rigid world of the neurodiverse, but it works both ways and some autistic people should perhaps make more of an effort to try and see things from a more neurodiverse point of view also; certainly the few phone calls I had via the Anna Kennedy website helped me see the whole aforementioned predicament in a more positive light. I've also been inclined to romanticise the episode somewhat by viewing it as a lucky escape; neighbourhood personality Joe Orton hadn't been so fortunate, some forty-odd years previously, but then again, I wasn't a prospering playwright and my friend wasn't a deranged, bald, disregarded muse either. One of these days I must get around to visiting that particular flat, where said playwright had his skull caved in by the aforementioned deranged, bald, disregarded muse.

At this point I feel that I must stress that I enjoyed many happy months in the Islington flat before the whole 'crack crisis' came to pass. The duration of my tenancy saw me through two particularly hot summers and a typical English winter with little in the way of snow, but the taste of independence was wonderful whatever the weather. For the first time in my life I really had the chance to grapple with the minutiae of everyday life, like paying bills and doing the washing-up and the hoovering; tasks most people undoubtedly deplore, but it was wonderful to be doing them in a place you could actually call your own. We visited my parents every Tuesday, taking my washing because we didn't yet have a washing machine, and also because in the early stages I often got quite homesick. The fact that we bundled Wolvie and Tiggy into the car for each of these visits now strikes even someone of my neurodiverse nature as faintly ludicrous, although it seemed perfectly proper at the time. I loved those two cats and simply couldn't bear to be parted from them. One time we were driving back over London Bridge late at night when a police car pulled up alongside and the female officer in the driving seat began waving wildly to us. We thought she wanted us to pull over for some undisclosed driving misdemeanour but in fact she was gesticulating wildly at the cats, pulling funny faces and trying desperately to catch their attention. On another occasion, Tiggy – considerably the more timid of the two – crawled under the passenger seat whilst we were pulled up at a garage in Catford. What followed was perhaps a full five minutes bordering on blind hysteria as we ran around the forecourt foraging for him, until he crawled out from under said passenger seat utterly oblivious – as cats so often are – to the concern he'd caused.

During my time living in Islington I became overly familiar – and also rather fond – of Barking, a town which was pretty much the polar opposite of the well-to-do neighbourhood so beloved by Joe Orton and the Blairs. Barking was – and I guess still is – basically your classic working-class East London hamlet, rife nowadays with racial divisions, but populated still with a plentiful supply of salt-of-the-earth cockneys alongside a sizeable immigrant population. The first time I visited Barking, it also boasted a 'Doctor Who'/sci-fi shop, secreted away in the upper echelons of the town's lone shopping centre, Vicarage Field. Dave drove me to Barking one chilly Friday in December and after I'd made my 'geeky' purchases we had a slap-up meal in the nearby Wimpy, followed by a brief wander. The shop – 10th Planet – held regular signings of fading stars from 60s, 70s and 80s 'Doctor Who', and pretty soon I'd formed a nice circle of friends from the people I met in the queues; mostly these events were held on Saturdays from midday onwards, and such were the crowds that it could take you three or four hours before you actually met the guests of your choice. Alongside this I also joined a London-based sci-fi group that met in a pub off Oxford Street, making several more friends there, a few of whom soon joined me at the Saturday signings; again, this was action prompted courtesy of the Anna Kennedy website, when I found myself bemoaning the fact that I didn't have much of a circle of friends to pick from. Several months later I found that I had so very many friends to pick and choose from that Gary – surely my BFF – became vocally quite jealous of all the 'strings' I had to my bow; 'But I don't even have a quiver!' I replied, in a moment of the utmost autism.

The Saturday signings in Barking soon became an anticipated regular fixture, this roughly around the time I was forced from Islington and back to the family home, thus serving to somewhat take the sting from that particular mishap. My little group on these occasions consisted of a civil servant called Neil (aforementioned), a City of London policeman called John (mordant), and an estate agent called Jamie (jolly); occasionally John's friend 'mad Michael' accompanied us, but that ceased when he and Neil embarked upon rather a spirited altercation whilst on the platform at Barking Underground, in the midst of a particularly lively debate concerning lecherous psychiatrists.

Swinging back to the signings themselves, well, after we'd met the 'celebrities' of our choice, we would then decamp to the 'Barking Dog' Wetherspoons pub over the road, spending the rest of the afternoon getting uproariously drunk and sharing anecdotes about our favourite 'Doctor Who' stories. Often some of the guests even turned up in the pub and joined us in our merriment; Michael Sheard, better known as 'Mr Bronson' from 'Grange Hill' was one, and Anneke Wills, 'Polly' from 1960s 'Doctor Who', another. One time I even collared someone from one of the old William Hartnell stories from 1964 whilst he was on his way home on the Underground after the signing, ignoring his repeated attempts to read his newspaper whilst John and Jamie egged me on from the opposite seat.

Now, it may not be politically correct to point this out, but within the confines of those star-struck signing queues, I often glimpsed a great many souls who – like myself – loved the making of lists, perhaps lacked a certain sense of social etiquette and who perhaps had a deep craving for a fairly rigid sort of daily routine. I guess what I'm trying to say is that if you're autistic you will never feel entirely out of place amongst a queue of people waiting to see a washed-up sci-fi star; it's just a fact. A sci-fi signing is also one of the few places where you can turn up clutching a crumpled carrier bag and looking like a piece of old toast and no one will think any the worse of you – I don't know whether they carry that kind of lifestyle tip on the Anna Kennedy website currently, but if not, well then maybe that's for the best.

As a postscript to this chapter, it's maybe worth mentioning that I recently won the 'personal achievement' award at the Anna Kennedy 'autism hero' awards, held in a swanky London hotel on a Saturday evening when my dad was on death's door in King's College Hospital. This sobering fact was underlined by my sister taking his place at the table, given that she'd flown over from Australia in case the worse came to pass, which in the end it didn't. When it was my turn to take to the stage, I made what passed for a brief speech, thanking my mother as '…the real autism hero', before hurriedly scampering back to the table and hoping that the earth would swallow me up. I think I looked pretty good in a tux, though.

As for Anna Kennedy herself, well, she was a lot smaller than I'd expected her to be, but I was still so star-struck that I couldn't even begin to elucidate all the times her website had helped me out; besides which, there were people literally queueing to have their picture with her, so the time spent orbiting her awesome sphere was actually pretty limited. Several months later I volunteered to help out at her 'Autism Expo' at Brunel University, running a clinic where concerned parents and the like could come and see me and then articulate their various concerns. I chatted to her mother-in-law in-between sessions and also with several of the women behind the organisation – Mala and Tally – explaining mainly about how I've tried to positively reframe my experiences in order to help people going through the same sort of stuff. Most of all, though, I take from that day the heart-breaking look on the face of the mother of one autistic boy, who sat there during my clinic fervently hoping that I'd help her little boy, like I was 'Jesus for autistic people' or something; by this stage I'd grown a beard, so you never know. I hope that what I actually said did help her out, though; as bad as it is for her boy now, it's still incomparable with the crap my generation went through back in the 80s. That was comfort to her at least; cold comfort perhaps, but comfort, nevertheless.

'L' is for...

...learning disabilities.

I'm afraid – as I've doubtless made abundantly clear – that I'm simply not logical enough to suss maths, and mostly I merely fumble around subjects like physics; harking back to the letter 'D', this chapter serves in some ways as an expansion on the whole idea of developmental delay. I also find simple reading rather problematic, especially with dyslexia merged into the mix (dyspraxia, as I've previously mentioned, is also prevalent among the autistic community, but that's another 'D' entirely). I manage my reading nowadays by moving a bookmark slowly down the page and passing it over each sentence in turn; if I don't follow that simple rule then the words are literally jumping around all over the place. Despite this I don't have much problem reading street signs, TV subtitles and the like, so maybe it's rather a selective form of dyslexia; either that or it simply doesn't bother when the words are blown up that big. I also struggled with the internet when first I came across it, around the time the world was wandering on into the new millennium. I should like to add here that some web designers really need to spare a moment's consideration when picking a font size for their websites, for those autistic people specifically struggling with the written word. For myself I've found it best simply to enhance the resolution, the words then becoming so clear that I couldn't fail to pick them out.

However, the internet – and particularly social media sites – remain a lifeline for autistic people, given the rather fraught social intricacies of face-to-face conversation. When I first began using a computer at home, donated from my dad's office and set up in our spare bedroom, well, back then there wasn't any Facebook or Twitter or Instagram; by the time I was boarding in Islington there still wasn't, but there were some websites with 'forums', where people chatted in various topic-based threads/posts. Pretty soon I discovered a website devoted to my favourite author, Anne Rice, along with an attendant forum. I hovered around on the peripheries of this forum for several months, sussing out the members and their lingo – cliquey didn't quite cover it – before I finally took the plunge. Although I'm often tongue-tied in the flesh, my natural aptitude/autistic 'superpower' for working the written word meant that I soon settled in pretty well. I struck up a correspondence with a girl called Catherine – 'Cat' – who lived in Yorkshire, and who was one of the few British members, in fact; most of them were Americans. Cat was a Goth, of sorts; also an epileptic and a voracious reader not only of Anne Rice but also various urban fiction authors, with a touch of Tolkien thrown in for good measure. Cat didn't seem quite your classic neurotypical, but she wasn't your full-blown neurodiverse either. Like me, she effortlessly juggled multiple obsessions, but she could also pretty much dispose of those she was done with, whereas I tended to stick to something I liked pretty much the entirety of my life thus far. Despite this, we hit it off so well that she came all the way down to Islington to visit (several times, in fact), although I found 'hosting' someone under my own roof without my parents around to help something of a strain. I wasn't quite aware of the responsibilities of a host and happily sauntered off to do my own thing on more than one occasion, before Dave quietly brought me up to speed on the whole etiquette of having a guest. It was during one of these visits that Cat and I met several other 'forumites' in the flesh, to see the film version of Anne Rice's 'Queen of the Damned' novel, in Leicester Square. I had my hair cut into a 'fashionable' fringe especially for the occasion. Afterwards we went for dinner, meeting up with one of the people involved in the actual scoring of the movie. He was friendly with Vanessa/'Vampvan', the girl who'd first started the Anne Rice website, and who later went completely off the rails and became a sort of psycho-stalker for one of the other girls, Rebecca/'Becky'/'Bitch Widget'. I don't remember having any of the usual autistic difficulties in regard to communicating with all of these dubious characters; Cat kind of acted as my chaperone, in a way. Even though the film itself turned out to be a bit of a turkey, I was so excited to see it up there on the big screen that it nevertheless helped me 'forget' about my various neurodiverse dilemmas for a few short hours.

I even ended up going to New Orleans with Cat, mainly for the purpose of hoping to meet Anne Rice, so that she might sign several of her books for us. Anne Rice lived in a big mansion in a 'posh' part of the city called The Garden District. Navigating your way around New Orleans could be rather tricky, because one minute you were towing the sensible tourist line, and then a block later you're the only white face in sight, and everyone else is staring at you like you're an alien or something. There was a place near the French Quarter called Elysian Fields, a sort of 'no-go' area peppered with shabby brownstones with groups of young black men hanging out front, leaning on rickety wooden porches and looking vaguely threatening. I went and sat with a group of older guys on one such porch and casually told them where I was from, before adding that I wasn't quite sure why I wasn't supposed to cross the 'safe side' of the avenue from the French Quarter to come and talk to them. They shrugged nonchalantly in response, one commenting that they didn't know quite why this prohibition was in place either, before offering me a drag on the rather hokey-looking joint they were sharing. I politely declined.

Whilst we were in New Orleans, Cat and I met up with another 'forumite' called Anne/'The Watcher', whom we then 'lost' – temporarily – during a French Quarter ghost tour. I say 'lost', because we didn't really lose her at all; she hit it off so well with Cat that I began to feel somewhat left out, and whilst Cat may have been slightly neurodiverse, Anne most certainly wasn't, and pretty soon the two of them were gassing away whilst I was left hovering around on the periphery like a spare part. Now, it was a perfectly beastly thing to do, but during this ghost tour I took the opportunity to leave Anne perusing some haunted gin palace or other whilst the rest of the group – Cat and I included – moved on. Anne soon lost sight of the tour group and wandered back to Jackson Square to wait for us. When we found her, I was forced to stifle my autistic penchant for telling the truth and basically keep quiet about the whole thing. Of course I felt bad, because Anne was really nice to me; therefore, when we went on a crocodile tour in the swamps I made a concerted effort that I wouldn't leave her stranded on some sandy bank with a pair of huge reptilian jaws lurching towards her; well, at least as long as she and Cat kept me in the conversational loop, of course.

During this trip, Cat taught me how to handle her if she had an epileptic fit, directing me to her website and its attendant 'Cat's Epilepsy Pages' as a point of reference; thankfully I never had to put any of the measures into action. I think she was worried about the temperature somehow bringing on an attack, what with New Orleans notorious for its hot, wet, sultry climate. I myself have never borne heat with the good spirits with which most people seem to bring to bear when the sun comes out. To me the hot weather makes you sweaty and irritable and unclean; unclean denotes disorder and of course disorder is anathema to your average well-ordered autistic soul. I quite understand that I'm in the absolute minority when it comes to drawing this conclusion, but I simply can't contain my hankering for the cool, clinically sterile comfort of winter.

There was a Scottish girl on the Anne Rice forum called Jeanne-Marie. She was quite vocal about many things, but especially about her blatant stalking of the 'Popstars' / 'Pop Idol' singer Darius Danesh; in fact, the level of her obsession almost put some of my own autistic ardency to shame. Although it's quite safe to say that none of the members were by their own admission particularly 'normal' – each and every one of them skirting around the fringes of society in varying ways – they were still a step-up from the vague but loveable transients with whom I'd consorted at the KFC at Marble Arch. Cat and I remain friends to this day but we were never destined to be all that close; our rather similarly selfish personalities clashed to the point where we would often find ourselves having rather public verbal disagreements, including in an aisle of Walmart in New Orleans, where we almost came to blows. Also, she was quite happy to 'slum it' in some youth hostel in New Orleans whereas I was more suited to the conventions of your average four-star boutique hotel. We also butted heads over my inveterate snobbery when it came to claiming the benefits of the copious free coupons she printed from online. Perhaps she wasn't even slightly autistic at all; she was too disordered to be autistic, and way too willing to strike out on her own, whereas similarly your average autistic person might be left crippled with insecurity at the mere prospect.

I was back living with my parents by the time I hit it off with Jane, another 'Yorkshire lass' living it up in the confines of the Anne Rice forum, although unlike the rather resolutely single Cat, Jane was contentedly married to Rick. However, passion had long since flown the nest and so she sort of adopted me as a surrogate husband; within months of meeting we were heading off to New Orleans on our own private Anne Rice odyssey. I think that was my fourth visit and we had to make several rather harrowing flight changes to get there. Although Jane was far more practical than myself, I was nevertheless her tour guide for this trip and thus once more vaguely shouldered with the sort of responsibility I'd felt hosting Cat; for instance, it was up to me to complain when the light fitting in our hotel bathroom began to leak, and it was me who had to arrange and plan each and every detail on our Anne Rice-related itinerary. Still, I like to think she had a good time, and over the years we also added Paris and Venice – during carnival – to our list of holiday destinations. Her husband was very welcoming to me, but when Jane split from him and had a tempestuous affair with her Romanian gym instructor, well let's just say that he was a little less accommodating of our unusual affinity. Jane divorced Rick and promptly married her Romanian gym instructor and as a result we now see a lot less of each other than we used to, and I miss her frequent visits to London greatly. She has a wonderful little daughter now called Clara, and a newborn called Emily, and so I like to think she's finally found some of the happiness that was missing from her first marriage, even though it appears to be at the cost of our friendship. She came down with Clara quite recently to meet me in Oxford, and for that one hot afternoon striding around the city with the two of them I could almost have sworn that I was just a normal man with a normal family. Almost.

I 'came out' to Jane regarding my autism whilst we

were watching the movie 'Adam' and since then – and before, to be perfectly honest – it's been 'our' movie. 'Adam' is a lot better and a whole lot more representative of people with autism than the cipher-fest that is 'Rain Man'; I made it about a half hour into that one before I had to just give up. I strongly recommend 'Adam' to anyone who wants to see a more heart-warming, balanced depiction of someone with autism, although the ending is somewhat bittersweet. Really, there aren't many movies about people with autism – especially adults – so you have to grab onto what there is out there with both hands. There are plenty more books on the subject, though, and even a comic book, published by Image and called 'Postal'; it's created by Matt Hawkins and Bryan Hill and well worth a look; and no, I don't know either of them at all, it's just simply that I love comic books.

Over the years I've amassed a considerable number of 'virtual' friends, mainly courtesy of the now-defunct Anne Rice forum. We exchange Christmas cards and birthday cards and communicate these days mainly through Facebook, almost on a daily basis. I've been visited by Rodney from Rotterdam and Anne from Finland, and as I said, I still touch base with Cat, albeit fairly sporadically. Rodney and Anne were both in one visit, and even though I didn't accommodate them I still had to 'host' the stay, given that they were coming to what was essentially my stomping-ground. We had a lovely weekend, all in all, dining in Soho and visiting the Tower of London, before taking in a 'Jack the Ripper walk' early on the Sunday evening.

I'd be lying if I said it was always plain sailing where the original Anne Rice forum was concerned, though. There was a big rift that erupted in about 2006 or so – petty differences and trivial tantrums – which led to a schism between several of the American and British members, and in which I myself played no small part. That spat led to the creation of the neo-forum on Facebook, which Jane and I still maintain pretty much under our own steam. For me, this forum – and Twitter – are, as I think I've said, a pair of social lifelines in an otherwise rather unforgivingly neurotypical world. I've found 'real life' friends falling away in recent years due to a variety of different reasons, whilst online people seem far easier to keep ahold of, and obviously to communicate with as well; it's less effort to talk to someone on the other side of a screen than it is to actually venture out into a harsh world and meet up with someone in the flesh. I know that's a sad indictment of the times that we live in, but I suspect for many adults with autism it's also something of a fact; heck, I think it might be a fact for a fair few neurotypicals too. I actually think I've gotten a whole lot 'more autistic' as I've gotten older, but perhaps this is simply a side-effect of coming out about the condition to so many different people, that perhaps one almost unconsciously plays up to the social persona thus expected of them. These days I tend to forewarn people about my appalling lack of eye contact directly after I've told them about the autism, but this tactic often seems to make said 'deficiency' all the more glaring. The same can almost certainly be said of some of my 'learning disabilities', whereby no matter how much I impress upon someone the fact that I'm able to grasp quite complex theories at the drop of a hat, the more mundane problems of everyday life often still leave me utterly confounded. In other words, I can pen a PhD, but I still have problems with tying my laces.

'M' is for...

...mainstreaming.

Mainstreaming refers to the idea that students with disabilities should be included/shoehorned into lessons alongside their more able-bodied/neurotypical peers. It worked for me on several occasions and then at other times/attempts it pretty much fell flat. I'd graduated from my Sociology BSc in 2003, a year later than planned because of the dreaded maths messing things up via the data analysis exam. Despite this setback I wanted to carry on being an academic forever – it can be done – although at the same time I wanted to write too, and so I decided to dovetail the two career paths, pitching some fiction to the directors of a creative writing course at Birkbeck, University of London. This was an MA course, a 'proper' class, if you like, as opposed to the unqualified class I'd taken some seven or eight years previously, under the tutelage of Paul Hallam. On the strength of my submission I went for an interview with the writer Russell Celyn-Jones; I was then offered a place on the course several weeks later. My confidence was further buoyed up by this acceptance, given that I was already on something of a high following my graduation. It only then occurred to me several years later that I might actually have been involved in a direct instance of mainstreaming on the part of my new tutors, given that I'd been rather frank about my 'misfortunes' during said interview. Still, this is only a supposition on my part.

I attended my first class – 6pm every Thursday evening – in one of the buildings overlooking Russell Square. I was perhaps the youngest pupil there, the rest of the class comprised of professional or at least semi-professional men and women in their late thirties/early forties, most of them wryly cynical but also secretly hopeful about the chance of seeing their stuff in print. This self-deprecating notion toward the possibility of publication had been reinforced a week or so previously in a kindly admonishment from Russell himself, during an en masse pep talk to the entire creative writing body. The gist of this talk centred around the fact that he thought it best to warn everyone that very few of us would actually go on to see our name in print, and certainly not to any degree of significant financial success. I guess he was merely trying to manage expectations, but for me it had the effect of shoving the proverbial firework up my arse; I became more determined than ever to see my books published, even though it would end up taking me a fair bit longer than first anticipated.

Returning to the notion of mainstreaming, my feelings/suspicions of inadequacy soon began bubbling, as I discerned the deep and meaningful subjects my classmates were writing about – journalism in war zones and the like – and there was I writing about the ghost of a debutante haunting a group of lusty barrow boys in modern-day Barking. My classmates were also very literate, prone to bouts of scoffing where the bounteous fortunes of writers like Dan Brown and JK Rowling were concerned. Everything for them seemed very intellectual, very wry and very arch, and absolutely sozzled with the aforementioned cynicism. Perhaps they saw my own modest literary efforts as a little light relief, I'm not sure. I like to think they were being genuine in their praise, but as an autistic person I'm often highly suspicious of neurotypicals simply because they rarely say what they actually mean; and to me, really, that must be an awfully constrained kind of a way to live a life.

Several weeks after the class began, I started shaping my various writings into an actual novel, concerning the aforementioned group of Barking barrow boys; that group eventually swelled into a large, sprawling family, one which still included the aforementioned barrow boys and also their debutante familiar. These works remain my pride and joy to this very day, even though they're a little like the literary equivalent of Marmite for those who have read them. An extract was published in 'The Mechanic's Institute Review', the anthology put forth by the class as a result of our weekly sessions. This hit the bookshops at the end of the first year of the MA, with me eagerly awaiting the calls from prospective publishers wanting to find out more about my work, although in the end my telephone turned out to be rather reticent when it came to ringing off the hook. The first among us to find publishing success was actually a quiet, bespectacled woman called Sally – her blog is called 'town mouse', so I don't think I'm doing her a terrible disservice – who secured a deal for a novel about birdwatching and murder some several years after we'd all graduated; I sat there during her celebratory drinks smiling but still slightly simmering because I hadn't been the first to find success after all. A rather sobering thought hit me just then, namely the rather unpalatable notion that other people might not actually find me and my work as fascinating as I myself found them; this was, I think, almost as equivalent a shock as that great Freudian moment when the little child discovers that the whole world doesn't revolve around them after all – I'm certainly still recovering from that one.

A year or so into the MA, I secured an extracurricular place on a week-long residential writing course held at a big cottage complex somewhere in deepest Devon. I made my own way there and was met at the station by one of the tutors, alongside several of the other applicants. Introductions were made – awkwardly, on my part – and off we were driven to the cottage complex in question. We were all given a run-down on how to manage ourselves whilst living at the complex, along with a rota of who would be doing what and when in regard to those times they weren't busy being creative. I wasn't too enamoured of the fact that I had to pitch in on various days with the washing-up and the cooking, but there was nevertheless a faintly pleasurable feeling of team building; I think also that dyspraxia and therefore the ever-present threat of dropped crockery featured somewhat in this reluctance on my part to partake in these particular chores.

For the greater part of each day we were left to our own devices – i.e. to actually write – and at various other times there were workshops and also a one-to-one tutorial with one of the two resident authors. These two women comprised a rather glamourous, knowing, faintly withering lesbian couple, all scrunch perms and short skirts and hardly what my inexperienced little mind thought a lesbian 'ought to' look like at all; I'd been permanently scarred by too much 'Prisoner: Cell Block H', perhaps. Every evening we all gathered in a barn beside the property and read aloud our works; of course, I couldn't do this, and I think I was the only one who didn't in the end rise up and regale their newfound friends with their lyrical prose. Instead, I sat there with my fists clenched, quietly hoping that our tutors would hop straight along to the person beside me; I vaguely remember someone else reading my stuff out for me in a show of pity, but the memory is hazy and perhaps

I was simply passed by altogether after all. My only really abiding memory of these barn-based brainstorming sessions was bearing witness to one of the lesbian authors flirting with one of the visiting female writers, whilst her partner/the other tutor looked on in ever-increasing fury. I didn't make any friends from the course, continuing as usual in being crippled by the same social anxiety that had scuppered my attempts at socialising during the great English language A-Level experiment of 1996. Despite this, I was however getting better at being around people and of partaking in the sorts of nonsensical small talk that seems so agreeable to mass gatherings. Having said that, I still had a way to go before I could consider myself to be in any way socially 'savvy'.

Prolonged exposure to the pseudointellectual atmosphere that seemed to percolate parts of the Birkbeck campus prodded me into taking what I considered at the time to be a rather daring step. Basically, I decided to 'come out' as autistic to one of the ladies on the creative writing MA. Her name was Tamsin and she was working on a novel about an autistic boy and his carers – without much confidence on her part, it seemed – and so initially I told her simply that I was in a similar position to the characters in her novel, albeit with the fib that I myself was actually the carer of a younger autistic sibling. I maintained this fiction for several months, until our two-year course came to a conclusion; I then came clean in a pub somewhere in the depths of Holborn, during an after-class drink; 'It's me!' I said delightedly, slamming both palms on the mottled wooden table that separated us, 'There is no younger autistic brother! I'm the autistic one really!'

Her reaction, it has to be said, appeared to me – to me! – to be rather a strange one. She got up abruptly and then she said, 'I have to go to the toilet.' Then, perhaps catching the look of disappointment on my face, added the caveat, 'It's not you Mickey, I assure you; I will definitely come back' – as though the girth of my lie were so great that her actually absconding from our conversation was in fact a distinct possibility. She did come back eventually, and we talked some more, but I can't really recall the gist of the conversation; we're still Facebook friends, so she can't have held it against me that much.

Another of my classmates was a dreadful, gum-chewing American woman with three or four MA courses under her belt already – 'What, does she collect them?!' sniggered my friend Sophie – who I overheard conversing with Tamsin on the subject of autism one evening. Whilst I sat there pretending to be doodling in the back of my notebook, this woman scoffed, 'Of course you know that some people say that children with autism are thought to be the children of the Gods, but of course that's absolute rubbish,' following which she cracked her gum, rolled her eyes and generally just stood there looking smug. I bumped into her a few years later on the Strand and she said that she'd email me and that we must keep in touch, but she never did. Apparently neurotypicals say stuff like that all the time; 'Oh, we must meet up! Oh, we must keep in touch!' but they never do. Or maybe they just say it to autistic people like me because they're trying to paper over the cracks of what for them was perhaps just a really awkward encounter.

Anyway, the point of all this is that I was starting to claw my way out of the autistic closet in a way I'd never considered before. This was helped by the fact that the topic of autism was also coming to the attention of the wider public at the time and the idea of an autistic identity was becoming more and more a viable option for those of us on 'the spectrum'; at least for those of us with enough coherent reason to determinedly make that decision. It has to be said that at this stage there still wasn't much to base such an identity on; I hadn't seen – and still have yet to sit through – the aforementioned 'Rain Man', which still seems to be the default setting for your average person's idea of what an autistic person is like. At this point I'd like to reinforce my recommendation for another aforementioned film, 2009's 'Adam', starring Hugh Dancy and Rose Byrne as the spectrum-crossed couple trying to make a go of things against a Manhattan backdrop. There's also a great film called 'Extremely loud & incredibly close' starring Tom Hanks, although the real star is actually the boy playing his 'autistic' son Oskar; again, a much more nuanced and realistic portrayal of what an autistic person is like compared to Dustin Hoffman's dreary, demoralising turn.

I also began seeking out the neurodiverse online, with varying rates of success. I happened upon the fact that some people were starting to call themselves 'aspies', after the Austrian Dr Hans Asperger, who'd made such inroads into the study of the subject; I'd once perhaps mentioned him in conversation to Nicky Crane. Personally, I can't stand the term 'aspie', and that hasn't much at all to do with the fact that Dr Asperger might have been a Nazi, but more simply that the fact that the word makes me think of snakes. All I know of Dr Asperger is that he was an Austrian paediatrician and theorist and to this day no one can quite make up their minds about whether or not he really was a Nazi at all. If people decide that he was a Nazi, well then, they'll have to change the word 'aspie' to something else altogether. For me it's simply the fact that, as I said, the word 'aspie' makes me think of snakes (think Cleopatra) and being autistic, my mind frequently fumbles these associative images, images that harden like quick-drying cement if I'm not careful, and then suddenly I can't shake them for love nor money. No, I prefer referring to myself for now as simply autistic; it's familiar and also it doesn't immediately make me – or indeed anyone else – imagine an Egyptian queen with a particularly sly snake in tow. It won't do much for the posthumous memory of Dr Asperger if historians confirm that he was a Nazi after all, but it would at least give those of us who don't much care for the name a chance to perhaps come up with something a bit better.

It was during this period of online foraging that I also found myself engaged – in the marital sense – to a rather stunning Canadian girl who wanted British citizenship. I – like so many of my autistic peers, in fact – was possessed of a quite astonishing level of naivety, and thought nothing whatsoever of the legal implications of helping someone out in such a way; rather, I was quite taken with the moral kudos of performing such a seemingly selfless act. It was only when Gary sat me down and explained to me the intricacies of any possible future divorce settlement that my position became a little clearer;

'You do realise,' he said, 'that if you get married and she then divorces you – once she has her citizenship – that she will be legally entitled to half of your belongings or estate or whatever it is they call it in legalistic terms.'

I shrugged. 'Well that's alright,' I said, 'because I don't really have an estate as such; I don't own a property or anything…'

'No,' he said, arms on the table, leaning forward and fixing me with his most serious expression, 'but she will be legally entitled to half of your Doctor Who DVD collection.'

I'm told that the colour quite drained from my face at this juncture. 'Half my Doctor Who DVD collection?!' I gasped, tugging at my collar with my finger.

Gary nodded solemnly. 'And that's just for starters,' he said.

I broke it off the very next day.

As a result of my online endeavours, I went on to attend a couple more neurodiverse pub nights, events that were apparently an offshoot of the Carnaby Street crowd I'd contacted via Anna Kennedy's website. These new gatherings were held mainly around the Holborn area, but I didn't particularly enjoy any of them; it might sound mightily offensive, but if you put a group of people with communication difficulties in a room and tell them to get on with it then you might be waiting a mighty long time to hear the first chinks of that ice breaking. There worst was one held in the foyer of the Barbican Centre, the less said of which the better; basically the organiser – autistic – sat us in a circle in this rather bustling public arena and then just let us get on with it; 'awkward' doesn't quite cover the ensuing fifty minutes of blank stares, garbled sentences and mumbled misunderstandings. How those poor bastards might ever have managed to mainstream on a daily basis was quite beyond me; certainly, I was finding it hard enough myself. I made a few more Facebook friends out of these meetings, but nothing steady. I still get invites to these occasions and sometimes I think, Yeah, I'll pop along there tomorrow night, but then the ghost of that mismanaged Barbican Centre meeting flares up and I opt for staying in with a DVD and the reassurance of my own quiet company instead. In that instance I suspect that I'm not entirely alone, that many autistic people secretly prefer the sweet reassurance of our own lonely reflection against even the company of our peers, provided in the roped-off area of a bustling City bar (or Barbican). Worse still, I guess, is trying to mask your way through an evening amongst a group of neurotypicals busily talking random creative writing theories; one can only mainstream so much, after all, before one is left feeling quite utterly exhausted.

'N' is for…

…NCLB, which stands for 'no child left behind'.

What this means – in greater detail – is '…to ensure that all children have a fair, equal, and significant opportunity to obtain a high-quality education. They should also be able to reach, at a minimum…proficiency on challenging state academic achievement standards and state academic assessments.' Now, NCLB was actually an American Act of Congress, but the basic mantra has since been adopted by some autism rights activists here in the UK. As for me, well, although I wasn't a child in 2005, I was however still waiting patiently for my chance to "…obtain a high-quality education". Now, clearly no one was going to re-enrol me back in school, and so therefore I decided that I was going to have to drag myself forward on my own initiative, on this occasion by applying to do a second master's degree. This time around I aimed for a place at the pointedly prestigious London School of Economics, better known in yet more 'abbreviated-speak' as the LSE. I was absolutely flabbergasted to find, several weeks after the fact, that my application had been accepted, and apparently without reservation; more mainstreaming, perhaps? On that basis I immediately began to worry – I'd declared my 'neurodiversity' on the application form – that they were really only taking me on in order to meet some sort of disability quota (I'm still occasionally troubled by the fact to this very day). I remember distinctly the first time I arrived at the disability office, observing the receptionist behind the counter observing me curiously as I sat waiting to meet the teaching specialist, her eyebrow raised in rather a dubious fashion. I tend, whenever I'm faced with that sort of reaction, to sometimes affect a limp or a lurch, occasionally topping it off with a little dribble, just for good measure; this helps people process the fact that there is in fact something 'wrong' with me even though they can't actually discern it. If you don't fake it thus then you might find yourself facing the accusation that you're a fraud; the flip side of 'cripping up', as they call it, is that you might then also have to endure being addressed in a sort of simpering, faux sympathetic voice, like people think you're as thick as two short planks or something. In that sort of situation, I think people fancy that they're being really nice and understanding – and of course glaringly inclusive – without realising how patronising it actually appears. As for 'cripping up', well that term mainly applies to able-bodied actors playing physically disabled characters, but it works well here as a simile about how autistic people – and people with invisible disabilities in general – sometimes have to ham it up in order to share in some of the same sympathy and understanding that their obviously disabled compatriots 'enjoy'.

Anyway, despite my misgivings regarding LSE receptionists, I steeled myself to the task of gaining another master's, purchasing a brand-new pencil-case and also a brand-new set of Muji notebooks (my autism adores their Feng shui simplicity). Several weeks later, I pitched up on the Aldwych and wandered warily up Houghton

Street, to start the first lesson in my Sociology MSc. Initially I'd enrolled full-time but pretty soon I changed to part-time when I found the rigorous schedule a little too relentless to handle. With hindsight I regret this decision, as it hindered my ability to make new friends, something that was bound to be difficult at the best of times; going part-time meant that you were only attending half the classes – sometimes even less than that – so the chance for striking up some routine familiarity with people was strictly curtailed. Having said that, if I'd tried to stick to full-time I most likely would've drowned under the workload, so perhaps it was all for the best.

It turned out that the LSE was a completely different kettle of fish to London South Bank, although both had 'celebrity' pupils in attendance during my respective stints, both of whose paths I crossed on several occasions (Louise Woodward and Monica Lewinsky respectively). But whereas South Bank was relatively relaxed and rather inspiringly ethnic, LSE seemed so much more uptight, with Houghton Street on any given day a veritable sea of white faces marching around like they had a bad smell under their noses. Maybe it's different now and maybe I was just there during a 'bad' year, but back then it did seem rather distinctly elite in a very upright and 'English' sort of a way. The buildings weren't all that grand, either; I knew something of the LSE's reputation and I was expecting wood-panelled corridors and great big dusty libraries, full of elderly professors smoking big curling pipes, but mostly it was just the same Formica and plastic-flooring that I'd found at South Bank; the same old juvenile graffiti on the toilet doors and the same old blank faces staring into the screens of their not-very-smart circa 2005 phones.

Without the benefit of Dave, Robin, Maggie, Richard and various others to buoy me up, I pretty much failed to make any real friends whatsoever during the whole two years I was at the LSE. There was a loose group that I hung around with, mainly in the wake of the dreaded data analysis classes, but we didn't go for drinks and we didn't exchange numbers; or maybe they did, and I just wasn't included in the equation. Despite what I just said about the Houghton Street vista, I do remember that some of this little group were in fact studying from overseas, whereas I'd come from the rather unexotic climes of southeast London; perhaps after all I just wasn't global enough to be part of the gang.

As a result of declaring my disability I was assigned a 'helper' who led me around the LSE library and helped me get the various books that I needed. I can't remember his name, but he was a really nice guy, almost insisting in his assigned role on accompanying me to the actual shelf in question and then plucking the book from said shelf on my behalf. Despite this help and attention to detail, I still felt a nagging sense of isolation; although the staff were made aware of my disability, the pupils were still painfully ignorant of the fact. I shouldn't have been particularly surprised, given that autistic adults are often overlooked even as autistic children are becoming ever more and more forensically understood; 'no child left behind' perhaps, but for autistic adults it seems quite another matter entirely, and please forgive me for returning to this particular bone of contention once again. I didn't feel particularly inclined to continue my journey out of the autism closet with my fellow students either, mainly because they always seemed so very preoccupied with their own 'global' concerns. Maybe I was also just that little bit too old to truly experience student life, you know, the whole drinking and living in halls thing, although to be fair most of my classmates were pretty much my own age; I'm sure my lack of inclusion was merely more to do with the fact that I simply came across as a somewhat strange, occasionally aloof, and on the whole a rather awkward individual. Overall, I'd say that my whole time at the LSE was a pretty lonely experience, and I think I talked to one of my tutors – Associate Professor Suki Ali – much more than I did any of my classmates. Even though I didn't directly tell her that I had autism, I sort of made it clear that I wasn't about to do any recitals of various postcolonial theories in front of the rest of the class in the way that one was required to do; she seemed quite happy with that, and in fact seemed almost to wink at the fact that I was the only one in that particular module who didn't offer up a presentation. I think she'd quite clearly 'clocked' that I was 'on the spectrum'; you don't get to be an associate professor at the LSE without having some sort of insight, after all.

Around this time, one of my beloved cats – Wolvie, from the Islington escapade, and named after the X-Men's 'Wolverine' – was knocked down by a car, on Good Friday 2006, and the fact that he didn't die outright from his injuries only made it even worse. Now, some people with autism have 'autism dogs', specially trained for various tasks besides the natural bond of companionship, and whilst this shows the affinity the neurodiverse have with their animals, for me it has always been cats. When I was little I had part-ownership of my brother's cat Pele, named after the footballer; I had no idea who the real Pele was, and my main lingering memory of this unneutered tomcat was when he scratched me, in the alley at the side of our house. Then came Anna, who disappeared mysteriously when I was around 7 or 8; fur and bloodstains on the wheel of my dad's yellow Ford Escort spelt out the secret tale of a tragic accident where she was concerned, I think. Then there was Julie, who had the misfortune to live with us during my tumultuous teenage years, including the period where I suffered the tongue of that terrible home tutor, Jim Alderson. Julie eventually 'moved in' with an old lady up the road but every year or so I'd glimpse her silhouette through the ribbed glass of our front door, peering in expectantly; I'd let her in and she would spend the day with us, sort of checking that we hadn't moved house or anything. At the end of the given day in question she would return to the old lady up the road; it was the sort of cheek that only a cat can get away with, really.

Not long after Julie 'moved' out, we heard a mewling in the garden, one dark and stormy night; when we went out to investigate, we found a beautiful white and tortoiseshell kitten whom we christened Emma. Initially my parents tried rehoming her with a lady in the next road – 'Mrs Fagg' – who was notorious for taking in strays, but Emma had decided that she liked the look of our place and was back pretty much within the week, working her way through the unruly allotment that separated our road from the next. She was only with us for a few years before she was knocked down, my dad a witness to the dreadful accident whilst I was busily gadding about in London, courtesy of Sight & Sound; I think that period was one of the few occasions when the welfare of a pussy wasn't the height of my priorities.

In the late 1990s, the old lady with whom Julie had taken up residence died, and so Julie presented herself to us one morning and proceeded to return home as though nothing had happened and no time had passed whatsoever; more hilarious feline cheek. By this time, we'd brought a grumpy ginger tom called Sam, whom Julie treated as an infernal interloper and avoided as best she could. I was most upset when she eventually died; up to that point it was the worst bereavement I'd ever suffered where a cat was concerned. Several years later, returning from Islington with Wolvie and Tiggy, well, an unholy triumvirate was thus formed, with the two newcomers quickly establishing an ascendancy over Sam and his mercurial moods. I don't miss Sam all that much because you just couldn't cuddle him or anything, but he was still a cat and I loved him for that if for nothing else.

Returning to the top of this tale, when Wolvie was

knocked down and killed I went totally to pieces; how I managed to complete my coursework at the LSE I'll never know. In fact, I don't think I even left the house for a fortnight; I barely ate, and I barely drank and for a while people were quite concerned about my health. We buried him in the back garden and I still go out there each and every night and say goodnight to him; to some people this might seem the absolute epitome of eccentricity, but it just makes me feel better and also like he's still around in some form or another. He was just about the friendliest cat I'd ever had, fearless and curious and playful, ready at the drop of a hat to come into the hall and chase his bouncing blue ball, the one that pinged so perfectly on the polished wooden floor. When he wasn't playing, he would spend ages simply cleaning Tiggy until finally he got bored of the task, at which point he would playfully bite Tiggy on the back of the neck and then stroll off, in search of more amusing distractions. No one who met Wolvie didn't adore him.

In the end I still managed to graduate from the LSE, with my extended network of aunties and uncles pitching up for the ceremony and also to help themselves to the vast amounts of free booze on offer at the reception. My brother was there too, and whilst I was flattered by the fact that he'd turned up, there's a picture of the two of us somewhere, corralled together at this post-ceremony reception and looking decidedly uncomfortable at the fact. I thought that maybe he felt a little awkward around me, but then recently he stood by whilst our mum wept as our sister made ready to return to Australia after one of her irregular visits, so I'm guessing perhaps he's not one to emote in public. However, he could certainly manage self-righteous anger fairly well, from what I can recall; there was an incident during my late teens when my poor mother, at the end of her tether because there was literally no support from the local health authority, called on him to help out in managing my behaviour. My brother and his wife duly sat me down and unleashed a modest torrent of admonishments in my direction, telling me in no uncertain terms that they weren't '...f***ing around,' and that I'd better behave myself or else there would be serious repercussions. Once again, so it seemed, people weren't discerning that I was disabled and that I myself wasn't getting any support either, at that point I'd never had any support, really. I was so disillusioned that I was self-harming at the time, my arms dashed with various little train-track nicks, but in their flow of self-righteousness they didn't seem to discern those either.

Special supportive allowances were, however, put in place by the LSE during the exam season, including the dreaded data analysis exam, but in the end it turned out that I didn't need the half hour extra time duly allotted. This was due to the fact that when revising I tried to encourage my mind to 'obsess' over the subject in the same way that I'd devoured every aspect of 'Doctor Who' as a little boy; however, it seems that you actually have to love a subject to gorge on it to that extent, autistic or not, and that certainly wasn't ever going to be the case where hardcore mathematics was concerned. Therefore, I took to copying down the most pertinent aspects of the topic into my Muji notebook and then just flicking through it whenever I had the chance; say, on the bus or just before bed, for instance. It worked for me, anyway.

My dissertation at the LSE, based around the idea of growing up 'different' in the 70s and 80s, and encompassing the various social and cultural changes therein – all this against a backdrop of the changing face of 'Doctor Who' – turned out to be so trim and well-presented that Suki Ali still passes it around to pupils even now, as a sterling example of how a decent dissertation should be laid out. One of the other tutors didn't quite get it though, remarking disparagingly that the show – 'Doctor Who' – had always in his opinion looked so very cheap and tacky; 'Yes,' I told him, 'but that's part of the charm!'

'What,' he replied, 'London facing alien invasion from a horde of pepper pots armed with sink plungers and egg whisks?!'

'But it's very British,' I explained, 'so surely you can appreciate it in the context of a social mirror, reflecting ideas of entertainment against a wider backdrop of a certain lost sense of British adventurism and eccentricity?!'

'Or perhaps it's just a load of old pap, eh Mickey?!' he countered.

Doubtless many of my classmates at the LSE went on to become wealthy bankers, whereas at the culmination of the course I was still adrift, 'cast asunder' once more into the world with an increasingly impressive tally of qualifications under my belt, but still not a half-decent job to call my own. Occasionally, I still knocked out the odd piece of clerical work for John Geach, and besides this I applied for several more jobs, hoping that the abbreviated 'LSE' on my CV might count for something, but whenever I was interviewed it appeared that my eye-contact was still crap and my social skills scrappier still, a doubt apparently confirmed when the inevitable rejection letter arrived in the post. Having said that, potential employers were nevertheless impressed by my educational resume and also by my various published works, but the sad fact was that I still lacked the hands-on practical experience required to hold down a professional position. To say that NT Me was frustrated by this lack of progress would be something of an understatement; in fact, we almost parted ways. I remember the occasion quite distinctly, with myself slumped at a bus stop on the Strand and watching enviously as various City sorts swaggered past, wielding their wonderful careers like batons with which to beat me about the head. Years had passed and yet there I still was, hopelessly hankering after the same thing I'd wanted since the halcyon days of Hackney Youth Workforce. I think maybe the fact was simply too much for my neurotypical alter ego to stomach, and as NT Me drifted away in the wake of those swaggering City sorts, well, I was forced to call after him, 'No child left behind,' abruptly bringing him to heel.

That summer of 2007 was also another of those dreaded occasions when life – as so often seems the case – was busy making other plans, whilst one is otherwise just breezing along rather nicely. My best friend Gary had fought off a particularly painful and vicious bout of bowel cancer in the summer of 2005 but in the spring of 2007, it returned with a vengeance; 'It's back', was all he said to me in the brief text following the diagnosis. Strangely enough it was during his period of grace from that grisly disease that I met someone who would turn out to be perhaps my rock from thereon. With hindsight it was almost as though fate were providing with one hand even as it ruthlessly gouged away with the other. For a while they – Gary and the incoming Steve Forster – knew each other, but in the year in which their trajectories overlapped they met just two or three times; it was as though they both subconsciously sensed that the latter was there to supplant the former. Sometimes that thought is positively chilling, but at other times it feels a kind of comfort. Both Gary and Steve were from Surrey, and from roughly the same immediate vicinity; yet more of an uncanny coincidence, at least as far as my vaguely superstitious, pattern-seeking neurodiverse mind was concerned.

I guess that although I was dubious about the success rate of 'no child left behind' – at least in regard to my own education – where the curing of illness was concerned, I most certainly didn't want any friends left behind.

'O' is for…

…OCD, or obsessive-compulsive disorder.

Now this one is a real nightmare, and I'm quite sure that a veritable truckload of people without autism would attest to that in a heartbeat. I've suffered from OCD to one extent to another almost my entire life, right from repeatedly washing my hands, down to muttering little mantras as I meander my way along the street, much to the consternation of my fellow pedestrians. Although OCD isn't exclusive to people with autism, it's my vague understanding that you're far more liable to develop this form of 'skewed' thinking if you happen to be 'on the spectrum'. Alongside the aforementioned habits, well, I've also opened and closed doors numerous times, turned lights on and off to a certain rhythm, and so on and so forth; I've even touched wood so often that the tips of my fingers got splinters. Eventually, the cycle of these various behaviours was broken, for one reason or another, although I can't recall what it was specifically that shook me out of it. I think perhaps on one occasion I simply missed the routine and then realised afterwards that there were no adverse effects, and thus decided to knock it on the head as a result. I think – as I've said – that I got over my panic attacks by following pretty much that same prescribed 'formula'; 'Oh look, I didn't suffocate or have a heart attack after all!'

I think the OCD began because I had such bad feelings toward the schools I'd attended; in fact, I was taken with such a degree of vitriol that I literally couldn't bear to go near them. If I had to get somewhere that involved passing one of the schools then I would work out an alternative route, usually a longer one, simply to avoid having to lay eyes on the wretched place. Maybe it was simply a matter of not wanting to dredge up unpleasant memories. However, when those bad memories persisted, well, then I would try washing my hands, often until the skin turned a rather fetching shade of ruby red. Sometimes the memories/intrusive thoughts would subside and sometimes they wouldn't, but always the overall horror remained of the calamity of possible contamination, either physically or somehow even psychically, that I might be 'infected' by the same unpleasant personality traits espoused by my former persecutors. Now, trying to explain this to someone without OCD can be a bit of a battle, but I'd always try and break it down to its basic logical components, usually by saying something like, '…well, would you really want to eat a cake baked by the man who once mugged your mother as she walked home?!' – and based on this argument, well, sometimes they'd get it and then sometimes they wouldn't. If the latter won out then I'd be forced to fling in ever more extreme examples, like suggesting that a taxi driver perhaps really wouldn't take a short cut past Auschwitz just to get his Jewish passenger to their destination on time, although then I'd feel bad for likening my experience to the horrors of the Holocaust. However, by that point the person that I was explaining OCD to might at least have gotten the general gist of what I was trying to say.

My incoming best friend Steve was somewhat understanding of this aspect of my behaviour, perhaps because he was a bit borderline OCD himself, although in the main this was confined to keeping the contents of his flat in immaculate, alphabetically-organised condition; to this day, he's the only person I know who actually catalogues his DVD/Blu-Ray collection into an exquisitely laid-out digital folder. Despite this, I wasn't exactly forthcoming where my autism was concerned; to him and then to his extended family I was simply 'eccentric' or 'unusual' or, in the words of his mother, a '…funny little fellow.' They've only recently had my autism explained to them, but we haven't talked about it as such; that's ok, because we don't talk about it much in my own family either; It really is the veritable elephant in the room. To the casual observer it might seem like my family are utterly disinterested in my autism – okay, admittedly my mum is no Anna Kennedy – but I think that's simply because they're from a different generation and also because – certainly on my dad's side – one simply does not discuss emotionally unpleasant subjects.

Anyway, Steve worked in the City of London as head of product development in corporate travel; he dealt with clients including some exiled European royals, as well as a famous model and several boyband members. He drank – sometimes copiously – in practically every bar within the Square Mile and had a life as ordinary as mine was utterly bizarre and disjointed. You might in fact say that he was living the sort of life that NT Me had always hankered after; namely, a good job in the City, alongside a stable and healthy family life and with a good circle of friends to boot. I was able to attach myself to his life in a limpet-like manner, allowing me to explore quite vicariously the very persona that NT Me would undoubtedly have approved of. I popped quite often into Steve's office at Broken Wharf House, down by the Thames, even joining him for drinks with various of his co-workers of an evening. On these occasions it was quite strange to meet people who'd simply gone to school, grown up and then gotten a job, in the way that 'life' had always said that you were 'supposed' to do. In return I think I served as a kind of a vague curiosity to them, someone who'd shirked the day-to-day drudgery of work for a prolonged stint in higher education, with no apparent time limits. They were envious, or so I'm told; how I scoffed at that, behind their backs; 'They don't know they're born!' I'd say, to no one in particular. I reasoned that they'd want my life for a day or two at most, but no more than that, surely.

One of Steve's work colleagues was a guy called Graham; Graham, with a glass eye nearly indistinguishable from the real thing. He'd been stricken with cancer several years previously and his eye had been removed as a result. I forgot this fact on several occasions when I talked to him, positioning myself on the left, from a point of view where he himself was basically blind; I would then return to Steve's desk and throw my hands up in the air in disgust, bemoaning the fact that Graham was ignoring me, or worse still, that he was giving me 'ableist attitude'. Graham was reluctant to talk about his glass eye, but I think he found my tactless neurodiverse approach rather refreshing; I asked enquired endlessly about the eye, about the ritual of taking it out and cleaning it before putting it back in and all sorts of other things that rendered Steve quite aghast when I regaled him with a potted version, after the fact.

I found it therapeutic simply being in the vicinity of Graham because of what eventually happened to Gary. When Gary's cancer returned it positively ravaged him, and by the end of 2007 he was dead; dead and cremated and completely erased from existence. In the years that followed, I found a strange solace from Graham having conquered the same terrible disease, still walking, talking and living, albeit with a wryly self-diagnosed dose of 'bitterness and darkness' thrown in. In fact, as the years wore on, I began to mould him into a veritable bastion of invincibility; a little bit of autistic OCD on my part, if you like, but most certainly from a wholesomely positive perspective. The fact that Graham was alive and well was something of a miracle to me when Gary was so utterly gone, and gone in such a grisly manner, at that. I used to feel immense privilege in just being able to sit and talk with Graham, to bathe in the wisdom of whatever it was he deemed fit to tell me. I'm quite sure he thought that I was a bit of an oddball, but eventually it filtered back to him that I had autism and then I think he had one of those 'Ah, ok!' moments, after which he understood completely. When I began to suffer from a rather odious form of OCD known as health anxiety, well, it was sometimes Graham to whom I occasionally turned for a pep-talk, given that he'd actually been there, pulled back from the brink of the same abyss that had swallowed up my Gary so ruthlessly.

Meanwhile, I was still busily bonding with Steve and further getting to know his family in the process. I was quite taken aback to see how close he was to them, close in a way that I'd never been with my own family, at least not since my 'troubles' had first manifested. As a youngster I'd been a regular at various family functions, but after that first senior school expulsion I'd made myself rather scarce, as people began instead to inspect me as though I were some sort of freak, rather than simply treating me with a modicum of concern. As the years passed, my immediate family began steadily to drift apart, mostly as the various cousins reached adulthood, moving away to make families of their own; or not, as the case may be, considering that a noticeable number of them don't actually have kids. Add to this the fact that some of them have since fallen out with each other to such a degree that all hope of a reconciliation appears nigh-on impossible, and that leaves me with a situation where quite suddenly I don't feel so bad in not attending any of the meagre gatherings still occasionally thrown. In fact, it sometimes feels like I need a scorecard to keep up with who's blanking who in my family, and why; this is almost entirely on my maternal side, I have to say. Certainly, it was never like this when I was little; back then everyone talked to everyone, and if ever there were any disputes then they were conducted behind the scenes, whilst on the surface everything remained sheer sweetness and light. Now, however, I find myself marvelling at rifts and disputes that have been going on for well over a decade, in some cases. I quite honestly think that some of the people involved in these various wrangles will go to their graves without having made their peace with the person they fell out with. Most notorious is my Auntie Barbara, who seems, bless her, to rather frequently put her foot in it; her sister – my Auntie Anne – hasn't spoken to her for several years now, ever since some drunken scene concerning a distant cousin and some items cited in a will, or something along those lines. Then you have Aunt Barbara's son Alan – my cousin – who so offended Auntie Anne's son Lee and his wife Lynne that they haven't spoken now for nigh-on seven or eight years, although that one may actually be around the wrong way altogether. On top of that, Lee meanwhile gave his mother – Auntie Anne – the silent treatment for almost a decade or more. You couldn't make it up, really you couldn't.

Eventually, I was invited to several of Steve's family functions, where I soon recalled that the neurodiverse tend not to shine at the dinner table, either drowning in a sea of crossfire conversations or else blurting out something so tactless that everyone literally stops and just stares. Steve's dad Bob was gruff and hypermasculine, whilst his mum was bright and breezy, and quite utterly past caring about her husband's often harrowing temper; 'You've never met anyone like me before, I'll bet,' Bob told me, brow furrowed into what Steve called the 'Forster stare'.

'No,' I responded, 'although, as the Americans say, ditto.'

Bob also had a dry, often sharp sense of humour. Sometimes I took some of the stuff he said quite literally, and his wife would end up having to caution him about the fact that I was 'sensitive'. However, because he himself wasn't at all sensitive, or so I reasoned, I considered him fair game for reprisals and would thus tease and wind him up mercilessly. It was then that he would employ that vaguely ferocious scowl – the aforementioned 'Forster stare' – normally reserved for roughhousing down at the rugby club, guaranteed to send most people fleeing for the hills; it certainly gave me the shivers.

I also got on well with Steve's sister, although we fell out briefly later on; her three kids seemed also quite affable, although I'm not entirely sure that they ever really knew what to make of me either; nothing new there then. Where Steve's non-work circle of friends was concerned it was worse still; I met many of them just the once and then suddenly they were making excuses about why they couldn't see him for a while, or else he simply met up with them solo-style. One of them was rude enough to say in my presence – but talking to him, like I wasn't even there – that just because I was his friend it didn't mean that she had to like me straightaway; we didn't see much more of her after that little outburst.

It was whilst meeting these various friends of Steve's that I also began to recognise the painful limitations of your average neurotypical conversation; so many subjects are off limits, or else they're discussed only once those participating have given themselves permission by imbibing large amounts of alcohol, and even then you've no real guarantee of full, coherent disclosure. I've never had that problem, and I know plenty more autistic people who can also spill the beans on any given subject at will, sensitivity/social norms be damned; in other words, never ask someone with autism if your bum looks big in this, because most likely the answer will be yes, 1) because they're being honest and 2) because it's a lot less boring than pandering to someone's forlornly fragile ego. This avenue of verbal sparring works especially well when you come up against someone who prides themselves in '…telling it like it is', these being the sorts who usually crumple the quickest when faced with someone else also willing to go the distance in terms of 'gobbiness'.

I became such a semi-permanent fixture around Steve's office that I'm sure a few people wondered whether or not I was hankering after a position of some sort (In a naïve way I was – on NT Me's behalf, mainly – even if it was just that of a downtrodden teaboy). The boss of the company was gay and he appointed several ex-boyfriends and various clubbing pals into positions of power, based on a sort of 'fruity freemasonry', so certainly there were precedents; this, alongside several other staff members setting up various spouses/siblings/offspring in certain departments. I mentioned this blatant nepotism to Steve, but he didn't really take the bait. I did quite fancy the idea of being teaboy for a week or two, pushing my trolley between the desks and dolling out sturdy mugs of decaf about the place; I wanted to belong, just for a little bit. Really, as I've said, I was just living vicariously through Steve a life it was increasingly clear I'd likely never have, sampling it by fraternising with his work friends, occasionally even skirting around the edge of office politics by virtue of osmosis. When dressed in my best smart casual V-neck sweater, with a periwinkle shirt beneath and some smart casual trousers down below, well, on those occasions I quite fancied that I really was just another daily commuter to the City, toiling away in some nice air-conditioned office perhaps close to St. Paul's Cathedral. But then, even in the midst of this idyllic dream, I'd often find myself slipping into the odd OCD routine, more often than not some horrible health anxiety woe or other. I hated it when this happened, but I sort of couldn't help it, and I guess that's what the 'C' in OCD stands for, although quite why you'd compulsively partake of something you absolutely loathe I'm still trying to discern.

'P' is for…

…perseveration.

This refers to the repeating of simple, routine tasks when quite clearly the need for performing said tasks has long since passed. You might consider this a vague follow-up to 'O' and all of those various horrors concerning obsessive-compulsive disorder, but for the most part perseveration is that little bit more benign, although possibly still quite irritating to those of a more psychiatrically based bent.

Clearly perseveration was very much the case in regard to the care that Gary was receiving, as he lay dying in a dismal side ward at the Royal Marsden hospital in Surrey, dying from an illness that was anything but benign. The doctors had sedated him heavily, seemingly stripping the need for those of us gathered at his bedside to try and reassure him with simple words, although we kept on doing so, even though it seemed – to me at least – that the need for performing said tasks had long since passed. The nurses said that he was never quite unconscious, hence the need to try and keep on repeating those simple, routine behaviours. Basically, they were asking us to perform continual acts of perseveration, talking to him and recalling old anecdotes and trying to draw his attention to the TV even when he was laid there with his eyes literally rolling up in his head. If he'd been a horse – or indeed any kind of animal – they would have put him out of his misery, but it seemed to me more like they wanted to wring every last drop of pain and fear out of him before he went. I couldn't – and still can't – see the point in putting a person through that when the doctors are so self-assured that there's no chance of recovery; if they are so self-assured of that fact then why bother prolonging the pain and the fear? It seems to me like one of those bizarre traits of neurotypical behaviour that the neurodiverse find so utterly incomprehensible; '…all life is precious', some doctor might say, to which I would reply, perhaps with the visual example of my best friend and his suffering at hand, 'What, even that?!' – so, whilst perseveration was high on the list of priorities for some, for me at least, during those last awful days of Gary's life, it seemed the least dignified resort of all.

However, because of the medical profession's seemingly rigorous aversion to dignity for the dying, I was forced to watch my best friend fumbling in and out of a morphine dream, staggering around in the middle of the floor on one occasion and then crouching down in a daze, seemingly about to defecate. On that occasion his uncle came to his rescue whilst the nurses merely milled around in the corridor outside, examining their cuticles. At other times Gary was lucid enough to talk to me and to make a morbid sort of sense about how he wanted his final days played out. He tasked me with finding and then composting his porn collection before his uncle cleared out his room, a task I undertook with a weary resignation utterly untouched by titillation. I remember dumping the lot – magazines and videos – in a big green recycling bin behind Steve's flat in Cheam Village; perhaps later on some of the waste-disposal guys helped themselves and had a jolly evening as a result.

Back at the hospital, Gary's family had gathered at the bedside to bid him farewell, although his close cousin Toni – she'd come clubbing with us several times during the Speed-fuelled heyday of the mid-90s – was curiously absent. From what one of his aunts told me, they'd drifted apart before he'd gotten ill and now she was a no-show because of guilt; I was a bit too caught up in the drama of the whole thing to pick up on the intricacies of the various family politics, but I'm friends with her on Facebook now, and we remember him fondly. Gary, meanwhile, was moved from one dismal side ward to another, before the decision was taken to transport him up to the Marsden's dreaded top floor, aka the palliative care ward. Once there, the doctors would finally show him a modicum of mercy by administering a heady dose of drugs that – so they assured the assembled onlookers – would '…send him peacefully to sleep.' Perhaps by then they'd simply decided that they couldn't possibly wring any more misery and fear out of him. I remember laughing that they'd bothered putting hand gel outside the wards on that floor; if everyone there was condemned to death then I couldn't see the point in trying to eliminate some bog-standard household germ from the equation. By now Gary was frequently vomiting faeces, a sight so horrific that even now my mind can't quite compute the fact. He apologised to me profusely for the grisliness of it all; I smiled weakly in response, cocking my head to one side and parking the joke we might in better times have shared regarding his propensity to talk shit. Both Dave and Steve hovered around on the periphery of this unimaginable horror show, offering help where they could but basically being about as impotent as the rest of us. Really, to mark your final days in the top floor at the Marsden was worse than anything the Tudors themselves might have dreamt up where a grisly demise was concerned; even the dreaded hung, drawn and quartered was carried out in a matter of moments, whereas Gary's death was drawn out endlessly over days and weeks.

Eventually I decided I needed a break, and so Steve drove me back to Sutton, dropping in to see our mutual friend, civil servant Neil on the way. We hadn't been there more than a moment before Dave called me, shocked and sobbing about the fact that Gary had just died. I wasn't shocked so much as slighted by the fact that my best friend had chosen to depart without me being there to hold his hand or something. It was only later that someone explained to me that quite often the dying wish to depart in a vague privacy, without their nearest and dearest gathered about the bed and bearing witness to every morbid moment; I later learnt that in those last moments Gary's eyes snapped open – so much for sedation – and an almighty torrent of excrement erupted forth from his mouth, like a deleted scene from 'The Exorcist'. Then he slumped back against the pillows, quite dead and past any more unnecessarily prolonged pain. Dave had rushed off in search of a nurse, although the one he found seemed particularly put-out by the whole thing, as though such scenes of horror were simply her bread and butter or something; to me it seemed that even in those final moments they simply couldn't be bothered to accord poor Gary any sort of dignity.

We went back to the hospital at once, gathering with Gary's family in the little waiting room where they shuttle through the various bereaved families; lots of tears and crying ensued, and even a few recriminations, from what I can recall. In those moments I was glad of the fact that I wasn't the only one who thought the hospital '…an evil place.'; it was a bit of a bugger that Steve's sister would end up working there, several years later.

A few weeks after Gary's death, I met up with his uncle, by appointment. He drove me down to one of

Gary's aunts, where we all of us met the vicar who was to conduct the funeral service. This man didn't know Gary at all and so I'd been brought in to furnish him with a few pertinent details, mainly concerning Madonna, with a few titbits about cricket tossed in for good measure. Hearing these anecdotes bounced back at me across the pews of the crematorium, several weeks later, as though the vicar and Gary had been best buddies or something, was just a tad unsettling. In fact, as the service progressed, I found myself far more focused on the vicar's vagaries than I was in bidding my best friend farewell. My mind appeared to be wandering a tentative track which viewed the vicar simply as someone paid to do a job, in the same way that those hard-nosed nurses had seemed like they were just doing a job; it felt like they didn't really care, in the same way that a prostitute doesn't really fancy you, instead simply pretending for the sake of the cash. Now quite possibly this is the kind of skewed, erroneous conclusion that only an autistic person might arrive at, or maybe – occasionally – it's one of those great unspoken truths that neurotypicals can't handle but which the rest of us process with relative ease. As I revisit this, with the Coronavirus ravaging the planet's population, I think I can safely say that the nurses and the doctors definitely aren't doing it for the cash; hats off to them, I don't think I could knowingly put myself in such danger. But that doesn't change the appalling manner in which my best friend died, and the apparent lack of empathy from the nursing staff thereabouts; there has to be a better way than that, surely.

Several weeks after the funeral, Gary's family were presented with a big, white and vaguely Tupperware-like container holding all of Gary's ashes. After the lid was peeled away, I for one was amazed to see how much ash and grit a melted-down human actually consisted of, not to mention how much that former person still weighed; I couldn't lift it up with one hand, basically. I was also disconcerted to see that it was indeed quite thick and grainy and not a fine powder, as I'd imagined it might be. His uncle was quite happy for me to take a portion of the ashes away for myself and I brought a nice container from one of the bigger ASDA stores in which to hold them. However, as the weeks progressed, I felt decidedly uneasy sitting in my bedroom and feeling Gary's presence poring over me as I tried to go about my daily duties; certainly, a blatant w*** was quite out of the question. Eventually I persuaded Steve to take custodianship of the container, but the same sense of unease prevailed even when visiting his faraway flat in Cheam Village. For a while thereafter my portion of ashes was consigned to the back of some random cupboard, where Gary's woeful/baleful presence might be a little less marginally felt. Eventually however I implored Steve to go and see Gary's uncle, with the intention of explaining the position I now felt myself in. Gary's uncle duly took back my portion of his nephew with good grace and said that he understood perfectly; certainly, I think the intimation seemed to be that he understood me and my peculiar ways as much as ever he had, but there seemed to be no hard feelings. We still exchange Christmas cards, but I never know quite what to say now that Gary is gone. It bugs me that the family harbour no ill-will towards the doctor who failed three times to diagnose Gary correctly, sending him off with a packet of 'Tums' on one occasion, whereas I would cheerfully throttle the w***** if ever I found him. To me it seems like doctors are on occasion a little like weather-forecasters; they get paid even if they get it wrong, only people don't die if you fumble on the prospect of a passing shower.

The stress of losing Gary, perhaps, caused me to develop rather a lethal blood disorder, some six months after his death; my platelets dropped almost to nothing and I was admitted to hospital as an emergency. Matters weren't helped when I was then casually transferred to the cancer ward without being told why, although it turned out that this was where the various blood-related maladies were also treated. Tests went back and forth but no discernible cause could be traced, hence a final diagnosis of ITP; 'Idiopathic Thrombosis Purpura', 'idiopathic' meaning no known cause. I was treated with a heavy dose of steroids, which certainly saved my life, although the side-effects – besides the dreaded 'moon face' – when combined with my autism, caused me to develop rather a severe case of steroid psychosis; let's just say that wrecking my bedroom was the least of it.

Over ten years have passed now since Gary died, and although I have Steve, I don't really still have a proper best friend to fill the yawning vacuum that Gary left behind. When you're autistic you tend not to make friends easily and Gary was like the crutch that I leant upon as I stumbled my way through the world. Recently my friend Jamie – the estate agent – also succumbed to bowel cancer, although we weren't as close and so from a purely selfish point of view, I was spared from having to see him depart this world in all that gruesome detail. I'm fairly sure that I shocked him when first he told me he was ill, though; I burst into tears and flung my arms around him, telling him how sorry I was, which probably wasn't the most comforting reaction in the world. I hadn't even known he was ill until that winter's day when I paid him a surprise visit, travelling from Paddington all the way up to his house in Marlow; when he opened the door the first thing I saw was the drip attached to his arm, with a little sack or something stashed in a sling around his shoulder; I think I knew straight away what it was and what it meant but I waited until he told me, over a cup of milky tea and a discussion about various 'Doctor Who' DVDs. Jamie's illness had initially manifested itself differently to Gary's and so I hoped it might therefore have a happier outcome, but that wasn't to be the case. Steve and I went to see

Jamie in St. Mary's Hospital in Paddington about a year after he was diagnosed – shades of Nicky Crane, although I resisted a 'nostalgic' revisit of the Rodney Porter ward – finding that he'd been divested of most of his bowels during some seriously major surgery. I tried my best to cheer him up, but he was understandably downcast; basically, he was the dismal shadow of his former cheeky self, and the discrepancy made me an uneasy visitor and himself an uneasy recipient, I think. That was the last time I ever saw him, although we texted a few times after he went home. His mum – 'Duck' – sent me a message on Facebook a few months later and said that the illness had come back badly, and that Jamie simply couldn't face the prospect of any more surgery or treatment, opting to go home to die instead. His funeral was a packed-out affair in a little church in Medmenham, complete with a Tardis-style 'Doctor Who' coffin and a vicar clad in a Tom Baker scarf. Several weeks after the fact, 'Duck' sent me another message on Facebook, this one remarking that Jamie would have been shocked to see that the new 'Doctor Who' was going to be a woman. I have to confess to being a little surprised by it myself – in fact the words '…it's all over now' lanced briefly through my brain – before I began to warm to the idea, mainly after I'd seen the little teaser trailer with Jodie Whittaker being unveiled to a waiting world.

Certainly, there have been times as a 'Doctor Who' fan when the art of perseveration has come in handy, watching the show even when the storylines were dire and I wasn't particularly taken with the lead actor either. But I had to keep watching, repeating that simple routine task because I'd been doing it my entire life. In fact, it's a bit like a marriage, devoting yourself to 'Doctor Who'; you tend to stick with it through good times and bad, through risible storylines, carping companions and all, right back around to when it was brilliant and the Blackpool exhibition in the late 1970s was just about the most exciting thing I'd ever seen in my entire life. I walked around that exhibition so many times that eventually the lady behind the counter came down and found me and gave me a complimentary ticket; 'You're here every day for pretty much the entire day,' she said to me, pressing the free pass into my hand, 'and we can't in all good conscience keep on charging you for the fact!'

'Q' is for…

…Q-CHAT.

Q-CHAT is a tool whereby the 'presence' of autism –
like it's some malevolent spirit – can be detected in
toddlers as tiny as 18-24 months in age. It uses a scale to
measure the sorts of behaviours a child should be engaging
in with their parents within that age range, and more
importantly where they're lacking, for want of a better
word. The autistic 'label' is then applied if the child in
question isn't interacting with their parents and with the
world at large in the way that it ought to be, in the way that
Q-CHAT *thinks* that it ought to be. Q-CHAT was
developed by researchers at the University of Cambridge,
and I guess it works wonders in helping the early diagnosis
of autism for those 'lucky' kids growing up nowadays,
when the sympathetic spread of awareness on the subject
is rampant.

I briefly considered calling this chapter 'quackery'
instead, but I didn't want to seem too dismissive of tools
like Q-CHAT; the experts are trying their best, I guess.
Such a diagnostic tool as Q-CHAT does make me wonder

what my life might be like today if it had been available back in the early 1970s. I certainly know that by 2009 my life was badly in need of just such a retrospective re-evaluation; my best friend was dead – new friends don't exactly fall from the trees when you have autism – and I was wandering from one MA to the next with only a vague idea of reaching the pinnacle of academia – a PhD – as a way of compensating for my conspicuous lack of schooling. I just didn't have access to the sorts of support systems that are available to kids growing up with autism today, having first been diagnosed as toddlers with the benefit of tools like Q-CHAT.

A lot – no, let's make that *the majority* – of autism research/campaigning/understanding is directed at kids. This is logical, I guess, because kids can't really fend for themselves against a world that fears and misunderstands them (Hello 'X-Men'). However, if you're an adult with autism then you might as well have the word 'invisible' stamped on your forehead in bright blue letters (blue because it's my favourite colour, besides being the default tint for a certain Autism charity dedicated to 'curing' the neurodiverse). There simply isn't any real support for autistic adults whatsoever; behaviours and traits that people often find charming in autistic children are just seen as odd or eccentric in the final adult version of said child. With the right support – via a Q-CHAT early intervention – I might have found a job and settled down in a manner that NT Me would entirely have approved of, but instead circa 2009 I had nowhere to go and no one to guide me, and so I simply started yet another MA. My old friend/sometime employer John Geach had died several years previously, so any chance of some more clerical work was out the window, along with his literally encyclopedic knowledge of the world and also his amusing habit of gasping, 'Shit and derision!' at anything modern and 'hip' that particularly shocked him.

For this latest MA I returned to Birkbeck after an

absence of some four years, this time to study gender and culture, with the idea of doing my dissertation on some aspect of the modern autistic identity; there was a promise in the curriculum that autism might be covered in one of the modules, but instead I ended up wrestling with concepts as opaque as 'the abject' and 'non-binary gender identities'. Some of it was fascinating and some of it certainly wasn't. Either way, it was fun watching the teachers jumping through their various intellectual hoops whilst I sat there, lolling back in my chair and trying to balance a pen on my puckered upper lip. My classmates subscribed to a general consensus of being 'hip' and tolerant, and yet they took great delight in slagging off one of the other girls in the class simply because she was breathtakingly beautiful but not particularly – or at least not obviously – all that bright. This animosity was passed off as a condemnation of her rather off-the-wall attitudes to the various subjects on offer – she was Russian – but I know plain old sour-faced jealousy when I see it. Another of my classmates embarked on an affair with one of the tutors, and besides that, another girl with whom I got pally dropped out quite suddenly, citing her personal misgivings concerning the general acceptance of the fluidity of various non-conformist gender identities. Yes, it was all very cerebral and overwrought, and yes, really often rather pseudointellectual.

I was directed to the disability officer at Birkbeck to get some assistance with my essays; his name was Marc and he was blind, but he didn't have the white, blank, milky eyes that blind people often sport on TV and in the movies. No, his eyes were brown and they darted about a bit, but they were indiscernible – to me, at least – from the eyes of someone who wasn't blind at all. In fact, as the weeks progressed, I became quite convinced that he wasn't blind; everything is very literal when you're autistic, and because it didn't correspond with what I'd seen on TV and in the movies, well, I simply wasn't buying it. During one of our later meetings I sat there idly gurning and grimacing, before half-stripping and pacing agitatedly around the office, waiting for him to gasp at the sight of it all. Only he didn't. I hurriedly made myself decent and then I went over and waved my hand in front of his eyes; 'What are you doing, Mickey?!' he asked.

'Dealing with my neurodiverse delusions,' I replied, before resuming my seat.

At roughly the time I returned to Birkbeck, I also joined a historical society concerned with the bygone minutiae of the East End of London. I was drawn to this by an undulating fascination with true crime – The Krays and Jack the Ripper, in particular – fused with a vaguely rose-tinted fondness for an England that had never really existed to begin with, probably. The society – The Whitechapel Society – met once every two months in a pub called the Aldgate Exchange, with a conference once a year, alongside the occasional one-day 'event' thrown in for good measure. I'd never been a member of a society before and therefore had no real idea about the petty personality politics that often rule and divide such a set-up; I was simply there to enjoy sharing my interest with like-minded people, but said personality politics soon reared their ugly head. For once, I was also able to enjoy being accepted for my encyclopedic knowledge of a subject rather than having the recipient of my enthusiasm raise an eyebrow and then race for the nearest exit. I venture to say that there were other members of this society who might have outshone me when it came to reeling off great reams of information concerning this or that subject at the drop of a hat, and certainly no one looked askew at them once they got started either. It was, if you like, a place where certain people congregated who'd somehow slipped through the cracks of mainstream society; don't get me wrong, they were – *are* – good people, but they were some of them...how shall we say, a little...unusual. And coming from me, well, that's really saying something.

The society also published a journal to accompany their regular meetings and it wasn't long before I was asked to contribute an article. For a while I even had my own regular column but then I ran out of things to say; there are only so many ways you can comment airily on the possible status of the Krays as cultural icons of the East End, for better or for worse. I also wrote some pieces about the society itself, channeling that strange propensity autistic people have for searing honesty to shine a light on the various cliquey corners. It wasn't long before people began seeking me out on account of these scattered pieces of prose; sometimes they would stop me in the midst of the bar and say, 'Someone said you were Mickey Mayhew – well I really like your stuff and your style…' and so on and so forth, to the point where my confidence really began to blossom. In fact, it grew to the point where I began writing about other stuff too, mostly in my spare time. For one thing, I continued that novel I'd been working on from my first stint at Birkbeck, concerning that great sprawling family from Barking and all of their various trials and tribulations, sending it out to various agents and publishers and basically trying my luck. At the same time, the committee of The Whitechapel Society sent a pitch to a publisher about an anthology; either that or the publishers contacted them, I can never quite recall, but in the end the offer was taken up and I was enlisted to write a chapter about possible Jack the Ripper suspect, Joseph Barnett.

At around this time, the personality politics within the society began really boiling over, with rival factions even going so far as to form a vague splinter group; pretty soon an actual schism had formed. Friendships forged over many years – including book collaborations – dissolved in the face of sparring East End tour guides and the like. Sometimes it got quite ugly, with people on one side sabotaging events set up by the other, leading to scenes of actual threatened violence at society meetings, which were real popcorn fodder for those of us caught on the sidelines. This schism continues unabated pretty much to the present day, and to be honest you'd need a flow-chart to keep up with all of the comings and goings of the various members, their torn loyalties and the like; a bit like my family, frankly. I've made good friends in The Whitechapel Society and I've fallen out with a fair few people too, simply because so-and-so said something on Facebook that so-and-so from the rival faction didn't quite agree with. This was one of my first experiences of the precious, easily-offended personalities that some neurotypicals nurse – and in fact seem to have to live with – on a daily basis; you get so used to being insulted when you have autism that it really can be 'water off a duck's back'. On the plus side, I made a really good friend in Christine James, a no-nonsense 'salt of the earth' Cockney sort with a bawdy laugh and a fairly tumultuous family background, who took a shine to me for reasons I've never quite fathomed. I always find, being autistic, that I tend to make friends with the most unusual people, people whom on paper I wouldn't automatically assume that I might end up being friends with at all. Whenever I started a new MA or MSc or whatever, I'd often look around the room and wonder who I might end up being friends with; as the years progressed and my wisdom widened I've since learnt to take a second look, realising that it will almost certainly turn out to be the person I'd least expected.

I didn't 'come out' in The Whitechapel Society as autistic for quite some time, and with Steve busily sanding down the rough edges from my various spontaneous statements, well, there really wasn't any need, either. In the end I only disclosed the information because I was working on this very memoir, dovetailing with my sudden 'obsession' regarding the idea of emerging from the neurodiverse closet; said revelation elicited a fond smile from committee secretary Sue Parry, a prim and 'proper' maths teacher from Norfolk. Sue had a penchant for sprawling, highly detailed and often elaborately structured anecdotes, stories that would often leave me utterly entranced as they wound toward their inevitable conclusion, usually replete with a last-minute twist or two thrown in. It turned out that one of her nephews was on 'the spectrum' and this served to soothe the way to a greater understanding of why my moods were so mercurial. In fact, there were several people to whom I 'came out' who then disclosed in return that they had this or that niece/nephew/cousin who was on 'the spectrum'; it's all becoming rather pedestrian, really, this autism business!

Anyway, the stress of dealing with the antics of the rival faction took its toll on Sue's health, especially where The Whitechapel Society's Salisbury conference was concerned; temper-tantrums and verbal tennis once more erupted on Facebook, disputes between various delegates soon spilling over into 'real life', often with quite sobering consequences. Facebook was by then a medium I'd pretty much mastered, and one which I now consider something of a lifeline, given the social isolation that autism brings. However, at the time of the conference it was pretty harrowing to be caught in the crossfire between these various individuals as they vented their sometimes highly personal frustrations back and forth across the screen. Sue hated Facebook with a vengeance; I think the dislike stemmed from her coming from a generation where you simply went and met someone if you wanted to say something to them, and cliques as a rule were something that only happened in the dingiest corners of your local coffee room. Despite everything, the Salisbury conference was still a success, but The Whitechapel Society was put off hosting another one for the time being because of all those toxic personality politics. I certainly had a nice time, although I couldn't quite see the particular charm of Salisbury; there was nothing to link it to any of my passions/obsessions, besides a house that Henry VIII and Anne Boleyn had apparently either stayed in or visited (my Tudor phase was well underway at the time), but the 'link' was a touch too tenuous for my liking. I was quite comfortable in the crowded conference venue, mainly because I pretty much knew everyone, so having my senses swamped by all of the noise and the bustle became a somewhat neutered risk.

I ended up having three chapters published in three separate anthologies concerned with the various suspects and victims of Jack the Ripper. One of these books was launched on one of the 'event' days organised by The Whitechapel Society, on this occasion held at the Crosse Keys pub on Gracechurch Street, in the City of London. It was quite something to have complete strangers coming up and asking me to sign their books for them, and better still to see the sales of said book rocketing up the Amazon charts, although I didn't make any money from these contributions; all profits went back into the society coffers, but for me it was all about the achievement. Several times I wanted to pick randomly one of my old schools and return there in triumph, waving one of these works high above my head; I wanted to say to them, How 'retarded' does that look to you, you judgmental f***wits?!?, only I didn't. You see, autistic people for the most part tend to be rather quiet, non-confrontational creatures. Instead, I merely sat back and enjoyed the praise from those who came and told me that I could write, that I had talent, and that it was clearly all quite something for a boy who'd been booted out of school at just twelve years of age.

Of course, maybe none of this aforementioned life would have happened if I'd been subjected to the rigors of Q-CHAT/'quackery' when I was a kid; maybe I'd have gone through school pretty much unmolested, securing a stable job and then settling down to some sort of a 'regular' existence. Or maybe it wouldn't have made much difference at all; I mean, telling whether a child is going to be autistic is one thing, but preparing them for the vagaries of the world at large is quite another. I guess it won't be long before even something like Q-CHAT becomes redundant, because eventually scientists will be able to locate/isolate the autistic gene and then…well that's a whole other discussion entirely, and one that I have to confess rather sends the chills down my spine. There's a hashtag that trends on Twitter sometimes called #endautismnow, one that's got a lot of people up in arms, what with those vaguely eugenic connotations; however, some people percolating around the autistic community actually argue that those on the extreme end of 'the spectrum' might really benefit from some sort of a 'cure'. You'll find as many people embracing their neurodiverse identities as you will parents lamenting the often-pitiable lives their children are living because their autism is so severe; one person's savant-like superpowers are someone else's socially crippling curse. Q-CHAT will probably tell you whether your child has autism, but it won't make them 'normal'/neurotypical; it does, however, give you a good heads-up.

Would that we'd all been so lucky.

'R' is for…

…repetitive behaviours and restricted interests.

Well, really, when it comes to autism, where does one start?!? One might also consider calling this chapter 'Vaguely nonsensical rules and how they don't apply to Mickey', as will become abundantly clear further on.

I do however take issue with the phrase 'restricted interests'; I'm interested in what interests me, so I'm not quite sure how that interest then becomes something society construes as 'restrictive'. Ever since I was a kid, 'Doctor Who' has always been my main passion and that includes watching my favourite stories over and over and over, until I can literally recite the whole thing verbatim; I know plenty of fellow fans who can likewise perform thusly, and who don't have a diagnosis to underline it. I also like going to 'Doctor Who' signings, conventions, exhibitions and all various other 'geeky' pastimes, and again I know countless people who also do this, people who – to the best of my knowledge – have no diagnosis whatsoever to dampen their ardour. These people certainly don't seem particularly restricted by the scope of their interest, and I don't much feel that way myself either. Now, if it was only 'Doctor Who' that 'did it for me' then perhaps I might be able to pass myself off as simply another geek, but as it is…

…by the time I was in my early thirties I was also quite obsessed with the Tudors (despite my aforementioned relative disinterest in Salisbury), with a particular penchant for the two 'tragic queens', Anne Boleyn and Mary Queen of Scots. This wasn't my first turn with the topic, however. When I was still in junior school, I became momentarily mesmerised by the subject, even taking to carrying around with me a copy of 'The Ladybird book of Henry VIII' wherever I went. As an adult I enjoyed the Showtime series starring Jonathan-Rhys Meyers, although initially I wasn't au fait enough with the subject to be offended by the various historical inaccuracies, preferring simply to enjoy it as good old-fashioned entertainment. Now that I'm a little more well-versed on the subject I *still* try to enjoy it as a slice of good old-fashioned entertainment, fearing that if I don't that I might come across like one of those dreadful po-faced historians who literally rips the entire thing to pieces just because the programme plays things a little loose with the facts. I've crossed paths with enough famous historians – certainly regarding Tudor times – to know that the phrase 'don't meet your heroes' is a very apt one indeed.

Because of the renewal of my 'restricted interest' in the Tudors, I visited the Tower of London several times, not to mention Hampton Court. In the latter location I was rather perturbed to find that some of the most important rooms were actually closed off to the general public. Now, most people would simply accept this and move on, but not me, not once I'd had a chance to take it as an opportunity to trample all over the various niceties of NT Me's social boundaries. I therefore promptly approached one of the wardens and asked them if I could have a look at the room where Jane Seymour – 3rd wife to Henry VIII

– gave birth to their son, the future Edward VI, as said room didn't appear to be part of the standard palace floorplan. The guy seemed so taken aback by the audacity of my request that he simply bowed his head and then led the way with a flourish of his arm, escorting me down a series of back corridors and then up a flight of sequestered stairs until we reached the room in question; 'We use this as a changing room for our costumed performers now,' he explained, watching me peer around the door, taking a few pictures on my phone as I did so. Now, sometimes that sort of sass works – i.e. asking to see a secret room – and sometimes it doesn't, but either way the results can be pretty spectacular, whether for good or ill.

This scenario happened again several months later, when I was visiting Holyrood Palace in Edinburgh, the main residence of Mary Queen of Scots. Her bedroom and presence chamber are open to the public but the supper room in which her private secretary David Rizzio was murdered by backstabbing Scottish nobles is not; the public are held at bay by a bossy little rope hooked from one side of the small stone entrance to the other. This time around, I began my gambit by addressing an innocent enquiry to the warden patrolling those venerable rooms, as to where precisely it was that the Scots queen took her suppers; he immediately unhooked the rope and let me scamper about the supper room for several minutes, although I wasn't allowed to take any pictures. Now, I'm not really condoning this kind of semi-brazen behaviour, but rather I'm simply citing it as a case of your average 'high-functioning' autistic person in action; despite the savvy we still have scant conception of social boundaries, especially when sure that no real harm will come of our enquiry if and when answered in the affirmative. It worked for me on both occasions and I got where I wanted to go, but I was still left with a faintly puzzled feeling as to why these precious, hallowed spaces were actually shut off from the public in the first place.

As well as being Queen of both France and Scotland, Mary Stuart also spent nearly nineteen years as a political prisoner in England, ferried to and fro between various castles and grand country houses whilst they tried to keep her out of mischief. One of the places in which she was imprisoned in England was Wingfield Manor, an impressive but now semi-ruinous structure towering distantly above the village of South Wingfield in Derbyshire. For a time, the place was run by English Heritage on behalf of the actual owners, with part of the site thus still serving as an actual working farm. By the time my 'restricted interest' had wrapped its hands around my throat, Wingfield Manor was entirely a private property once again, still a working farm but with a strict 'no visitors' rule now applied. In fact, the word 'visitors' is something of a gentle misnomer on my part; substitute the word 'trespassers' instead and you have more of an idea about what they thought of the average historian ambling up there to have a poke around. Steve drove me past the place several times and we soon found some strategic points in the village where you could get a really good look at the building. Pretty soon after that we also found a driveway that led down to the edge of the wood skirting Wingfield Manor; the signs regarding the actual starting point of 'private property' were a little hazy around this side of the village and so I decided to take my chances, following some dog-walkers and simply hoping for the best. Pretty soon I was veering off the established path and working my way slowly uphill along various narrow, grassy inclines, occasionally catching a glimpse of one of the worn red-brick towers of Wingfield Manor in the distance. I clambered over a stile and bypassed a trampled barbed-wire fence and then quite suddenly there it was, looming over me, with merely a small stretch of waist-high grass between us. I soon found my insolent progress somewhat impeded, however, as said grass was dappled with an almost invisible dew that rapidly left my lower half almost drenched. I slouched, quite sodden but also quite unfulfilled, all the way back to the car, and thus off we drove. However, as kismet would have it, as we left South Wingfield, we passed the village hall where the local historical society was holding an exhibition. Somehow or another Steve got talking to an old couple whose house was situated almost directly opposite Wingfield Manor, on the main road in and out of the village; the husband – Peter Wall – promptly offered to drive me up there and introduce me to the owner. Of course, Steve was all for leaving well alone and not troubling these kind country folks, but the offer had been made without any bare-faced neurodiverse needling on my part and so I gladly took them up on it. The man who actually owned Wingfield Manor was a farmer called Sam Critchlow; he lived alone in a ramshackle house incorporated into the ruins, with only his Alsatian guard dog 'Mary' for company/protection. I was given carte blanche by Sam to potter about the place almost to my heart's content, whilst Steve was invited to tea by the Walls, enjoying cakes and various finger foods back at their rather spacious and strategically well-appointed house.

Naturally, I couldn't be contented with exploring the ruins of Wingfield Manor just the once; no, on my insistence we made friends with the Walls and encroached on their hospitality several times, with Peter taking me up to Wingfield Manor in his Landrover whilst Steve waited patiently with Mrs Wall. I think some boyish part of dear Peter rather enjoyed these little excursions, during which he'd regale me with childhood tales of playing in the ruins as a child; I would nod and smile at what I thought were the appropriate pauses in his recollections, coming off as quite the neurotypical, so I thought. Steve and I also did a 'proper' English Heritage guided tour of the site after Sam Critchlow eventually agreed to a partial reopening. It really was a wonderful place, full of roofless great halls and sycamore trees growing askew through the shattered walls, but I went there so often that literally I exhausted it, and now it doesn't figure much on my radar at all. The same might also be said – sort of – for Chartley Manor in Staffordshire, which was Mary's penultimate place of imprisonment before she was executed at Fotheringay Castle in Northamptonshire. We'd been warned off visiting Chartley Manor by several sources, but after my success with Wingfield Manor and the Walls, well, I wasn't about to be deterred so easily. Chartley Manor was shrouded by trees and a moat and was fairly inaccessible even from a peeper's viewpoint by virtue of being situated alongside a busy A road. The 'Private – keep out' signs were still fairly sporadic, which meant that we were able to drive around the back and park in the fields surrounding the manor house without being challenged; the remains of the older structure of Chartley Castle were visible on the hills adjacent. Steve stayed with the car whilst I strode through the corn and wheat to see if I could get a better look at Chartley Manor. I took several pictures from the far side of the moat and then clambered all over the remains of Chartley Castle before finding myself confronted by a farmhand wielding a shotgun; 'What's your business here then?' he asked, rather gruffly.

'I'm looking for Mary Stuart,' I replied.

He scratched the back of his rather sunburnt bald head; 'Reckon she's been dead a couple hundred years now,' he sniffed.

In fact, he was pretty polite about the whole thing, telling me that I was trespassing on private property even as he apologised for the fact that the signage wasn't all that clear. It was the perfect moment in which to play on my autism, to claim ignorance of neurotypical norms and all that, but I didn't. Instead I took his admonitions on the chin and strolled back to Steve at a leisurely pace, with the friendly farmhand bringing up the rear, rifle aimed rather unsteadily at the heft of my rump. After that incident, Steve refused to drive me there ever again and as I myself can't drive and the place seemed miles away from any train or bus route, well, that was that. To this day I still haven't gotten a good look at Chartley Manor, and as my 'restricted interest' in Mary Queen of Scots has rather withered I'm not sure that I ever will either. Most of the time I don't even give the place so much as a second thought, but occasionally – like now, when I'm writing this – my peculiar brain will be reminded of the fact that one of my 'restricted interests' passed by partially unsated…

I was, however, more successful where Dunbar Castle was concerned. The battered remains of this once-mighty fortress sit atop a seagull-infested outcrop adjacent to the harbour, discreetly roped off for the most part but in some spots with actual lines of steel fencing in place to keep the curious at bay. The steel fencing speaks to the fact that Dunbar Castle is even more ruinous than Wingfield Manor, crumbling away in great chunks into the brutal North Sea at regular intervals. It's the place where the Earl of Bothwell took Mary Queen of Scots after he'd kidnapped her, and where he then 'ravished' her, as so many of the history books say; others will say that she was in on the kidnapping and that she and Bothwell were in fact star-crossed lovers. Given the air of mystery percolating about the place I simply had to experience it, so we located the harbourmaster – Bob – and he opened up the steel gates and took us up there, on foot, 'health and safety' be f***ed. There were yawning great gaps in the stonework as we ascended, and through them you could see the rocks down below with the waves crashing against them, the sound punctuated regularly by the shrieking of the seagulls. It was exhilarating.

Given my past predilections, it was obvious that I wasn't going to be satisfied with going to Edinburgh just the once either; no, I had to go again and again and again – actually 'repetitive behaviour' doesn't quite cover it. As soon as my Tudor passion crystallised around Mary Queen of Scots, I literally had to visit every spot concerned with her until…well, until I'd gotten it out of my system, I suppose. On top of that I had to read every book about her that I could get my hands on, including obscure, voluminous texts some several centuries old; I had to watch every movie, TV series and documentary too. Really, I had to know *everything* about her, and I simply couldn't bear the thought that there might be some nugget of information out there that I had yet to assimilate. Now, for someone whose neurons don't fire in this particular formation – most neurotypicals – understanding this sort of 'repetitive behaviour'/'restricted interests'/obsession may be a little difficult, but to the neurodiverse, well, such a passion can become so all-consuming that it overrides almost everything else. Sometimes said passion will continue unabated for several months, or sometimes even several years, but eventually you will probably reach a place of burnout. Now, burnout usually occurs when you've read every book, watched every movie and visited every place associated with your current particular passion/obsession, and usually more than once, at that. If you have nothing else waiting in the wings then what follows can be a period of relative frustration as you regurgitate your former spent passion, trying desperately to wring a few last drops of excitement from it before it fades altogether, and you experience full-on cold turkey. As I've grown older I've learnt to observe this peculiar pattern and moderate my behaviour accordingly, so that I can rein it in a little if I want to prolong the shelf-life of a particular 'restricted interest'/obsession beyond a certain span of time; less is more, and all that.

As a result of my mania for Mary Queen of Scots, I also joined The Marie Stuart Society, an organisation devoted to promoting – with some serious panegyric – everything concerning Mary Stuart, although the committee insisted on using the French version of her name, making it likely that their organisation would probably drift past your average Google search. They had both a Scottish branch and an English branch, but I would say that the majority of the members were Scots. Most of the members were retired, which meant that as I sat in the back row of the various society talks, I gradually grew accustomed to the sea of blue-rinses and shiny bald pates stretching out before me. The society was run by a formidable woman in her seventies called Margaret; imagine well-coiffed white hair and a regally purring Scottish accent, her every financial move scrutinised by Ian, her fastidious accountant of a husband. Most of the members were also cut from this similar cloth; conservative middle-class sorts hailing from well-to-do St. Andrews or else some other affluent suburban sprawl, normally scattered around Edinburgh's outskirts. Steve and I stuck out like a sore thumb amongst them, but not as bad as poor old Cindy Kilar, an ageing transsexual with a 'look at me' megaphone of a voice box. When she spoke, it was like a sudden shout or a yelp in a room otherwise punctuated merely by the odd polite murmur. She seemed to be tolerated by members of the society more than she was actually liked, but I did my best to get past the bluster by engaging her in some typically straightforward neurodiverse small talk, hoping that she would respond warmly to a fellow outsider. On that basis I went straight to the heart of the matter, asking her, 'Are you a transsexual?' – followed in fairly rapid succession by 'How long for?' and 'What do your family think?', before finally the inevitable, 'But are you still...well, you know, *anatomically* a man?!'

Now people either take this direct line of questioning rather badly or else they warm quickly to someone who doesn't appear to be your average neurotypical bullshitter. Cindy opened up rather readily, telling me all about being disowned by almost her entire family, living on a virtual pittance, taking overnight coaches to and from the various society visits, alongside having to eat cheap remaindered salads in order to save her few remaining pennies. Several years later I was able to show her a little more kindness by giving her a signed copy of my Little Book of Mary Queen of Scots, but when I first met Cindy the fact of being an actual published author was still a fair way off; back then I was still working my way towards it, submitting my stuff over and over again and simply hoping for the best; more 'repetitive behaviours', and all that.

'S' is for…

…stimming or 'self-stimulatory behaviour', which really isn't as rude as it might sound.

Stimming involves the repetition of certain verbal or physical tics; said repetition usually serves to bring about a feeling of relaxation and calm for the (autistic) person performing them. However, the sight or sound produced by someone stimming might very well grate on – or at least serve to unnerve – your average neurodiverse; in public it might be relatively simple to distance oneself from the 'stimmer', but if stuck with them in, say, the confines of an exclusive cinema, well then that might be another matter altogether. A small group of professional film critics discovered this fact the hard way when they found themselves ensconced with my good self for a screening of the Catherine Zeta Jones film 'The Rebound', at the Courthouse Doubletree Hilton near Carnaby Street. I was there because I'd answered an ad in a London lifestyle magazine, in the hope of procuring the position of resident film reviewer; doing endless degrees costs a lot of money and I needed to finance my academic renaissance somehow. I was given 'The Rebound' screening as a try-out, wherein I proceeded to sit through the entire movie whilst gently tapping/stimming my fingers into the hollow roundel beside my seat, the spot where one normally puts a drink; I did it so enthusiastically that the famous film critic Mark Kermode tapped me on the shoulder and told me to stop it at once. I introduced myself when the screening finished, marveling at the fact that Vanessa Feltz was sat a row or so behind us; 'Oh, she'd turn up to the opening of an envelope,' he said tritely.

'But she's put a gown on and everything!' I replied.

Mark Kermode shrugged. 'Some people really love envelopes.'

My review of 'The Rebound' was published in the lifestyle magazine several weeks later and on that basis the position of resident film reviewer was formally confirmed – secure employment! NT Me was ecstatic, even though I myself saw it merely as a means to pay for the aforementioned return foray into higher education. A few weeks later I was sent to review the Drew Barrymore rom-com 'Going the distance', at the Warner Brothers offices near Holborn; I took Steve with me as a treat but neither of us particularly enjoyed the film. In fact, we were the only ones present in the small private cinema and thus I was free to 'stim' without fear of censure, tapping my fingers and sometimes even rocking back and forth in the executive leather chair in a slow, rhythmical fashion. The preview screenings came thick and fast following on from that; I saw 'Scott Pilgrim vs the world' next, at the Empire near Piccadilly. By then I was becoming quite familiar with the faces of my fellow reviewers, but I was still so cack-handed when it came to starting a conversation that there was scant hope I'd actually become a comrade-in-arms. I never again saw Mark Kermode, however, or even Vanessa Feltz; maybe she was busy opening other envelopes.

The next film I saw after 'Scott Pilgrim vs the world' was the pseudo-comedy 'Vampires suck', at the Apollo

Cinema at Piccadilly; the press screening was at nine or ten in the morning, a faintly ridiculous time to be watching a film of that ilk, but I couldn't really argue with the finery of the job description. After each of these screenings I would wander along Shaftesbury Avenue with my laptop and check into the Café Milan to write my review; I liked to send it off as soon as possible, in order to show my employers what a pro I was, and whilst the film was still relatively fresh in my mind.

When I reviewed 'Easy A' at Sony Headquarters in Golden Square, we – myself and my fellow reviewers – were treated to a champagne lunch beforehand, with some fancy nibbles thrown in for good measure; after several Pimm's I staggered down to the Café Milan in order to pen the review, which, despite the alcoholic fug in which it was written, somehow still got published.

Sometimes I would get the call to go and see a film at ten o'clock at night or something, literally at the drop of a hat. For instance, I was out drinking with my classmates from Birkbeck when I was rushed off to see 'Due Date' at the Odeon Leicester Square; I tapped out the review on my laptop on the last train home, making sure it reached my editor before midnight. I cannot remember for the life of me what that particular film was actually about.

I became so good at penning these pocket-sized movie reviews, and so diligent in sending them to my editors ahead of schedule, that I was waylaid by the adjacent theatre columnist to do some reviews for him on the side. Pretty soon I was ensconced in the Etcetera Theatre on Camden High Street and watching something called 'Next!'; again, I have scant recall of the thing, apart from the fact that it was a one-woman art performance, a piece I unfortunately didn't find particularly enthralling at all. I do however remember that I began quietly stimming in order to occupy myself, mumbling a few careworn mantras and then tossing my pen from hand to hand in order to mediate the stultifying boredom. In fact, I became so enthralled by this simple, subtle motion that I lost track of the art performance completely, up there on the makeshift stage before me. I ended up missing so much of the play that I had to email the venue a few days after the fact and request a synopsis, so that I might appraise myself of all the scintillating details that my stimming had deprived me of first time around.

The next film I saw was 'How do you know' at Sony Headquarters, followed by a couple more at various locations, before the work began to dry up a bit. Eventually word went out that the magazine was knocking its film and theatre reviews on the head, and so quite suddenly my lucrative little side-line pretty much evaporated before my very eyes. I have to confess that I didn't much miss being asked to go and see some random movie at the drop of a hat, but it was still a shame; I'm a bit like Teflon when it comes to jobs, it seems. Still, it was something pleasant to put on my ever-expanding CV, and certainly if nothing else the experience taught me a little about the dangers of stimming too exuberantly in a public place.

Nowadays I tend to keep more of a handle on my stimming; I have a coin that I keep handy which I flip up and down for simply ages until the urge to fumble with something recedes. Elastic bands fascinate me somewhat in this regard, also; I like to stretch them as taut as can be and then snap them back onto the tips of my fingers, or else around my wrist. Apparently, some people with various anxiety disorders keep an elastic band around their wrist at all times so that they can 'snap' themselves back to the present when mental trauma looms. I'd like to point out that I don't think stimming is similar in nature to a compulsion or an obsessive-compulsive disorder because it brings pleasure and relaxation to the individual and not anxiety and unrest. I think that for the autistic person, stimming serves as a distraction to the overwhelming stimuli of everyday life, or at least that's how it feels when I'm doing it. I still stim to this very day, for what it's worth, almost always using the aforementioned coin.

At roughly the time my burgeoning career as a film reviewer was coming to an end, so too was my latest master's at Birkbeck. I completed all of the coursework without too many problems and graduated with a reasonably good pass. I quite liked some of my classmates and wanted to stay in touch with them but for the most part I think they had other ideas. It was at times like this that the social gulf between the neurotypical and the neurodiverse became ever more painfully apparent to me; to this day, I still see pictures of my former classmates on Facebook, socialising with each other, and stuff. I try not to be too bitter about it, but there are times when I wish someone would rinse out my psyche and scrub all of the autism away, just so that I could enjoy a normal, balanced social life. I wish occasionally that I could join in and laugh at things that I might otherwise consider rather flat or uninspiring, simply so that I might be a part of the crowd; any crowd, come to think of it. But one guest – i.e. yourself – is all that you're allowed at a pity-party, so there you go.

I was still socialising with Steve's family at the time, but all that went down the pan when his sister, now working at the same hospital where Gary died, said that someone had accused the nurses there of being a bit rubbish and a bit neglectful. This was at a pre-Christmas drinks, unfortunately. I happened to concur with what this other party had said but I bit my tongue until the day after, and then sent her a text where I gave vent to my frustrations. We didn't speak for several years after that, if memory serves; the neurodiverse really can nurse a grudge for a lifetime, believe me. However, I spoke to one of my tutors about it recently and she told me that it all concerned 'intent', that Steve's sister hadn't intended to offend me, which reminded me of the time when Dave became a crack addict and inadvertently caused me to flee the flat we'd been sharing, a wrench I'd also eventually forgiven. We were able to put it behind us in the end, and I think that eventually she understood that I often processed stuff quite differently to the way that 'normal' people did. It was rather sad, because for the most part I got on with Steve's family rather well. His mother's best friend Terri made me a 'Tardis' birthday cake once, the blue icing she used causing my poo to emerge resembling little nuggets of Lapis lazuli. When I saw this I naturally panicked, convinced that I'd been struck down with some sort of deadly disease, until someone made the connection between the cake decoration and my toilet 'troubles'. This poor lady – Terri – died several years later and it was her son who then raised concerns about the nurses who had treated her at the Marsden, which *then* led to the disagreement with Steve's sister.

All of this was a great shame, because I thought that I'd always gotten along okay with Steve's sister and also with her three kids, even though we had little in common; their marathon family gatherings, for instance, starting in the early afternoon and then continuing until midnight or more; mostly I simply couldn't keep up, certainly not where the drinking was concerned, at least. Alcohol and I don't tend to mix all that well at the best of times, as I think I mentioned back when I was chronicling my escapades with Robbie. For starters, my face flushes and my heart beats really fast, alongside which there's no real release of inhibitions because I never really had any to begin with, never having really felt self-conscious about stimming and the like, sober or otherwise. This alcohol-fuelled release of inhibitions was, as I've previously mentioned, something I'd become painfully aware of when first I began meeting Steve's various friends; they drank to relax and to release inhibitions, but all I got from the experience was that racing heart beat and about as much autistic tact on my part as if I'd gotten completely sozzled. Having said that, I do have a weakness for certain brands of 'alco-pop', because they're sweet and because you can literally drink four or five of them and feel only fleetingly tipsy. The mania for wine has passed me by completely, although it can be amusing to watch people getting excited over a cheaply priced bottle at the off license, or else the opportunity to nip over on the ferry to pick up large quantities from various Calais hypermarkets. I guess drinking perhaps really is little a bit like neurotypical stimming, in that sense.

'T' is for...

...theory of mind.

This refers to the ability to discern your own thoughts and feelings and then to become aware of the fact that your own thoughts and feelings/desires and dreams are not the same as someone else's. Autistic people have great difficulty when it comes to confronting the fact that there is a whole world outside of their self-contained and often rather rigid little bubble of existence. This might sound a bit harsh, but believe me, I speak through arduous experience. It is of course fairly obvious that everyone is the centre of their own universe, but this is considerably more so when that person is autistic; autism is a very self-involved condition, but no blame for that should be laid at the door of the autistic person themselves; that would be akin to blaming someone in a wheelchair for the fact that they can't manage stairs. Because of these barriers, it takes a great deal of self-awareness and discipline on the part of the autistic person to cultivate an understanding towards their neurotypical neighbours, to see that their own psyches are as special to them as the autistic person's own well-developed inner world is to themselves. Recognising this bias on my part came at a rather ironic time during my long academic renaissance.

There was only one way to go after completing my latest master's, and that was to perform the ultimate academic accolade of getting myself a PhD, or a doctorate, if you will. Doing a doctorate means you have to focus on one single subject to the absolute exclusion of all else. You have to take yourself right out of the mind-set of the many – theory of mind – and insert yourself back into the fantasy world of the few; right back to autism basics, in other words. Therefore, the recognition of this unintentional bias came for me at the perfect time, the most apt opportunity possible to dip my toe back into the somewhat self-obsessed world of the seriously autistic. The subject I picked for this decidedly singular approach was my beloved Tudors, and more specifically the enduring fascination with Anne Boleyn. I loved Anne Boleyn for a myriad of reasons and so I decided to set out from that basis to try and see why everyone else considered her so fascinating as well. I was pretty sure – given the vagaries of human nature – that there was a vaguely morbid aspect to the whole thing, i.e. the fact that she'd had her head cut clean off, but I was prepared to park that theory for a while and see what else my research turned up before I began pointing fingers.

I applied at London South Bank University, somewhere that I felt both calm and comfortable after the occasional pseudointellectualism of Birkbeck and the somewhat snooty airs of the LSE. Continuity – a notion positively cherished by the neurodiverse – was maintained when one of my old teachers, Shaminder Takhar, agreed to become my PhD supervisor. Shaminder had taught me during my undergrad degree, heading some module or other that I couldn't quite remember, but I could certainly recall being rather intimidated by her, if not entirely spellbound by the subject at hand. There was something stern about her, even a little acidic, but she seemed to have softened somewhat when I returned to South Bank all those years later. However, the rules of academia stated that there must in fact be two tutors for a PhD and not one. I was filled with apprehension about who this second tutor might be. I wanted it to be someone else from my halcyon days, someone firm but fair like Ruth van Dyke or maybe Gaim Kibreab; the latter had called me 'lazy' but this was always said with a twinkle, a stance that certainly might have made my school days somewhat easier, if only some of those teachers had given me a little more leeway.

My second PhD tutor was a woman I'd never heard of before, someone from the culture department called Jenny Owen. She was practical and meticulous and not at all used to my little autistic tics, whereas Shaminder had a fairly good idea of what made me work and how best to digest my little off-the-cuff remarks. Despite this, the first few tutorials were rather terrible affairs; I couldn't keep up with the social tennis of talking to them both at the same time, throwing my glance one way and my words the other and never really getting up a good rhythm on either score. In fact, I became increasingly flummoxed as to how your average neurotypical ever managed it. It was so complex that it seemed to me like some sort of unattainable art form; 'How do you think I did with Jenny?!?' I would ask Shaminder, in the wake of a particularly taxing tutorial; 'Do you think she likes me?!' and so on and so forth. Finally, I confessed to Shaminder that I was actually on 'the spectrum', and that keeping up with the two of them was practically blowing my synapses. She promptly arranged for me to get some extra help with my tuition and in the meantime set about informing Jenny regarding my 'troubles'. Up until that point Jenny herself had been frustrated by my inability to grasp some of the key concepts vital to penning the perfect PhD, but in the wake of my confession to Shaminder she became much more sympathetic. Rather than her issuing me vague instructions, I informed her that a list of precise commands would produce far better results on my part; in fact, my desire for a concise list of 'to-dos' became something of a running joke between us. Over the next few years I had several solo tutorials with Jenny, discovering among other things that her partner was a rather prolific writer of true crime; I looked up his book that very evening when I got home.

In the meantime, I attended a conference on Anne Boleyn held at Blickling, in Norfolk. The actual venue was Blickling Hall, where most historians seem sure Anne Boleyn was born, before being transplanted down south to the fairy-tale confines of Hever Castle. Steve and I stayed at the nearby Buck's Arms hotel, literally adjacent to Blickling Hall, thus enabling us to simply stroll over the road each day for the various talks and events on offer. I was able to hand out flyers to the various attendees detailing the requirements of my research, making some valuable contacts as a result. I also met several high-profile historical authors, most of them perfectly pleasant but one or two sporting their notoriously prickly personalities with some apparent relish. I grew rather fond of Norfolk, so far removed as it was from the senses-battering bustle of London. Occasionally I imagined myself retiring there and living in some little thatched cottage in a field in the absolute middle of nowhere; a week or so later my mania would resettle once more upon Mary Queen of Scots, and I would want to retire to somewhere in deepest Derbyshire instead. Sometimes I would even want to see out my days in Marseille, where Rimbaud finally cast off his 'soles of wind'. I actually managed to work Mary Queen of Scots into my PhD by using her as a 'compare and contrast' angle with the fandom following Anne Boleyn; it was sort of shoehorning, but I was utterly at the mercy of my neurodiverse desires.

We also visited Cromer while we were in Norfolk, a place that I found fascinating simply because it was literally so quaint, like time had just stopped there circa 1975 or something. We also visited the Boleyn family church at Salle, a very small village boasting this semi-ruinous and rather creepy building with big brass plates scattered along the nave, wherein the forebears of Anne Boleyn were variously interred. I was torn between a morbid desire to touch them and also a desire to recoil violently, chock-full of a vaguely superstitious awe.

It still took me a lot longer to complete my PhD than I'd originally planned; I signed up for three years full-time, but it ended up taking me twice that with all of the various stops and starts along the way. It seemed that even the accolade of attaining three master's degrees were as nothing compared to the complexities of penning a PhD; always the dreaded prospect of passing merely with an MPhil – an 'MFail' – was dangled over my head as a means to spur me on to greater feats of academic prowess. Against this backdrop of myself correcting various methodologies sat the fact that Shaminder's mother was seriously ill and not likely to live long; increasingly our tutorials touched upon this almost as much as the fact that I couldn't get my head around how properly to pen an analysis chapter. I told her all about Gary and how I wished that I hadn't seen him in those last awful days but that I'd had a duty to be there as his best friend; she concurred, saying that quite simply she had to be there for her mother even though they'd enjoyed rather a fractious relationship over the years. Sometimes I wondered why I'd asked Shaminder how her mother was, because I hated talking about matters of mortality; apart from rekindling memories of Gary, it also served to remind me of my own fallibility and of the fact that one day I myself wouldn't be around, pulling myself along the pavements of London with my wonderfully gawky gait. It was theory of mind all over again, really; it was the right thing to do, often asking

Shaminder how her mother was, because I hoped that I could offer some advice based on my own experiences, despite the fact that in some senses I'd really rather not have known.

In fact, ever since Gary died – and certainly exacerbated by the ITP - I'd been suffering on and off from reoccurring bouts of health anxiety – sort of like a high-end version of hypochondria – that could on occasion be almost crippling in the severity of their attacks. Always the thought plagued me that some dreadful disease would befall me, and my life would ebb away because of the incompetence of some doctor, for whom the offence would be overlooked on account of what I often perceived as the casual freemasonry of the medical fraternity. I couldn't banish from my mind the fact that Gary had gone to the doctors several times with his stomach complaint before it reached crisis point and he was rushed to hospital; I imagined some mole or bump being overlooked on my part until it was too late, and the doctor involved simply washing their hands of any culpability whatsoever. Although I would confide my fears to Steve's colleague Graham later on, initially it was Steve himself who bore the brunt of this often-crippling condition. My autism had a part to play, seizing on this desire to keep myself from harm and turning it into another obsession, albeit one framed in a much darker hues; there was nothing of the hobby about this whatsoever. When I wasn't satisfied with the explanation of one doctor I would go to another, and when I wasn't satisfied with that explanation I would either look up my symptoms online or else seek private medical advice, often wasting money I didn't have in the process, a debt that soon began to spiral on my credit card statements. Often the fear would arise ahead of some momentous or joyous occasion; before holidays or Christmas I would fear the arising of some malady or other and thus go checking myself for various imaginary problems. When I confided my problem to people, I sometimes had a reaction that seemed a little like theory of mind, only in reverse; they simply couldn't put themselves in my position and understand that I couldn't reason these irrational thoughts out the way that most people might be able to. In the end I kept it mainly to myself, weary of the bemused reactions bringing up the subject often got me. There was a nice nurse in St George's Hospital in Tooting who told me that it was just a blip and that I would get over it; I ended up there several times thinking I was dying of this or that, on one occasion even on Christmas Eve. It was the absolute pits, really it was.

In the end I sought professional help, signing up for a series of cognitive behavioural therapy sessions, travelling once a week come rain or shine – mostly rain – to a house in Parson's Green where I poured out my woes to a kindly counsellor called Mark. He taught me how to use CBT to analyse these 'intrusive thoughts' and how to recognise them for what they were; the trick is to let the thoughts float by and not to engage with them, which is a damn sight trickier than it sounds. It's a bit like trying to carry on walking down the street whilst nearby there's someone calling you all sorts of rude names, deliberately trying to egg you into a reaction. Of course, my mind wasn't doing quite that; it was simply a survival mechanism malfunctioning. As part of the therapy I had to try and conquer the fact that I couldn't even say the word 'cancer'; in fact, not only could I not say it, but I couldn't abide it on TV or in books or anywhere else whatsoever. Who would want to talk about a thing like that, I reasoned, which was partly why I'd fallen out with Steve's sister in the first place. To try and illuminate this further, well, I know a fair few people who react strongly when confronted with evidence of animal cruelty; 'I can't bear it, just please shut up!' is an oft-used response in such cases, and it was simply the same with me where cancer was concerned; it was miserable, and so I just didn't want to know.

To some extent these CBT sessions 'cured' me of the condition, but I still have occasional flare-ups, often in times of high excitement or anxiety. I don't think my autism caused the condition because quite a few people suffer from it, but I'm certain my autism exacerbated it somewhat; the trick I guess was for me to turn the flawed obsession toward being an obsession for ridding myself of the flawed obsession, if that makes sense. Therefore, I didn't go to pieces quite like I might have done before the CBT when Jamie was diagnosed with the same cancer that killed poor Gary. Or maybe it was just the weary resignation of welcoming in more misery, regardless of however much I might have wanted to keep my little autistic bubble sealed off from such things; quite possibly some theory of mind there, I'd say.

'U' is for...

...under reactivity to sensory input.

This is in many ways the mirror of the letter 'H' and that chapter's whole issue of hyperresponsiveness to certain stimuli. And yes, it's quite possible for a person with autism to be 'stricken' with both. Under reactivity to sensory input basically means that a person with autism who has perfect hearing might sometimes appear as if they are stone deaf; they may also have a heightened tolerance to pain but occasionally exhibit an extremely low threshold for even the slightest of grazes. On any given day – and feeling somewhat hyperresponsive – the slightest verbal stimuli might lead a person with autism to cover their ears and wish that the noise might evaporate, whereas if they were under reactive on the same day in question then they probably wouldn't notice if an H-bomb went off just adjacent.

I basically became under reactive when it came to sending out submissions for the novel I'd been working on. After having an extract from said novel about my big, sprawling family from Barking published in Birkbeck's

'The Mechanic's Institute Review', I began sending out submissions on a fairly regular basis. The majority of these came back with a sort of bog-standard rejection letter – basically taken from a template – with your name scrawled across the top and then the name of the literary agent in question scrawled along the bottom, in a vague attempt to make the whole transaction appear human. However, several of them actually got back to me with a request to see the completed manuscript. Now I'd gotten a bit carried away where this book was concerned – a sort of literary stimming, if you like – and the word count for the novel turned out to be a whopping 672,493 words. Now, to put this into some sort of perspective, 'War and Peace' has a word count of a 'mere' 561,093, so to say I'd gotten 'a bit carried away' is actually a misnomer; rather let's be more accurate and say that I'd completely plunged into this fictional world that I'd created, to the exclusion of all else. In fact I became so under reactive to outside stimulus that I wasn't watching much TV, wasn't even eating properly, as I recall; Gary had chastised me at the time for not coming out so often, because he was still around when I first began working on the thing.

Anyway, because of this corpulent word count I found myself with something of a printing dilemma when it came to answering these various requests for the completed manuscript. I sent the required first three chapters as a sample and then hoped they'd be so wowed by what they read that the matter of the word count would simply evaporate when it came to consulting the complete manuscript. I met with a literary agent during a reading at Birkbeck by my successful friend Sally and was given an appointment to drop into the agent's office with a view to discussing the possibilities of my debut novel. I wondered for days beforehand whether or not to forewarn this woman about the fact that I was autistic and that my eye contact and conversational skills might be somewhat lacklustre, but in the end I decided to brave it out, hoping that she would be too dazzled by my work to notice. Perhaps, I foolishly wondered, I'd be put before an entire publishing panel, with editors and cover designers and the like all thrown into the mix. In the end it was just me and her sat in her office, with a fine drizzle pattering against the window over her shoulder, the dull cloudy sky beyond doing its very best to bedraggle me. She asked me how the novel originated and why I had become so enamoured of Barking to the point where I'd written such a gargantuan tome about the place. As I'd included the local 'Doctor Who'/sci-fi shop in the novel I used that as a starting point for trying to frame my passion, but it fast became clear that either I wasn't being particularly eloquent or else she simply wasn't finding herself all that taken with what I was saying.

'It's so wonderfully working class over there in Barking!' I said.

'Working class is good,' she nodded.

'And, well, they're the salt of the earth, really!' I went on, 'and they'd give you the shirts off their backs if you asked them to!'

'Uh huh…' she nodded, making some sort of a note on the pad in front of her, '"…the shirts off their backs.".'

'That's right! They're proper cockneys! I mean, well, a few of them might actually be a little far-right in their leanings, but…'

She looked at me blankly, an eyebrow raised. 'Proper cockneys, huh?'

It was my turn to nod. 'Apples and pears!'

'I'm sorry?!'

And on and on it went; diverging courses doesn't quite cover it. I went away and then sat back with bated breath to see if I would hear from her again, but I never did; in the end I chased up our interview and she sent me a brief couple of lines in which she said that '…on further consideration' she had decided that she didn't quite 'get' the novel and therefore couldn't take it up with '…a clear conscience'. I thought that was a kind of weird response; I wanted her to publish it, not sleep with it behind her husband/wife/partner's back. However, I knew enough about wanting to be a writer to recall that if you were rejected then you simply had to pick yourself up off the floor and keep on submitting. Therefore, I decided to keep any mention of my autism out of the submissions and also banned any mention of the word count. These rather taciturn tactics led to me meeting an agent who almost bawled me out when I told her that the book I'd so enjoyed creating was in fact longer than 'War and Peace'. She suggested that a massive edit was needed and that several major characters and subplots would need to be completely excised in order to make the thing workable. It was at this point in the exchange that my eyes just sort of glazed over and I knew that I was experiencing a severe case of under reactivity to sensory input; I just couldn't hear what she was saying, the way she was being so blasé about me having to prune my literary baby in such a brutal fashion. All sorts of euphemisms for the process of creative writing careered through my mind, about how writing a novel is sort of like giving birth, basically the sort of literary froth that one often finds swirling around the creative writing community. I think in the end I just sort of stayed glazed over and told her that I would get back to her when I had had a good think about her suggestions; needless to say, the book is still sumptuously bloated, and all periphery characters are still alive and acting out their various subplots.

In the end I decided to indie publish the novel on Amazon; no outlay was required whatsoever apart from getting a cover together, although it was suggested by Steve that it might be wise to cleave the novel into three in order to make it more manageable, as well as to stop the cost of the paperback from spiralling. Maybe if I'd been a bit more patient with one of the literary agents then this outcome – the cleaving – might have been settled upon after some sincere reflection, but even so, I certainly wasn't about to cut any of the characters or what I considered to be those aforementioned essential subplots. I wanted the book intact exactly as I'd written it, in that one huge creative spurt, and that's how it ended up being published, albeit after I'd cut it into those three parts; 'Jack and the Lad', 'Taking Tiffany' and 'Jamie's Big Bang' are still on Amazon to this day and I've sold several thousand copies so far. It's been a real learning curve going down the indie publishing route, but the industry positively erupted at around that time and it seemed like a no-brainer; also the Kindle format was fast superseding the physical book, although this preference sort of seesaws depending on which news article you might be reading at any given moment.

It was around this time that Steve took it upon himself to contact the lady who'd commissioned the three anthologies for the Whitechapel Society, all of them eventually published with my chapters included. He talked it over with me beforehand, planting a seed in my mind whereby he thought I might try my hand at writing a book about my autistic passion of the moment, Mary Queen of Scots; he would then pitch the idea to the lady on my behalf, thus avoiding any potential social misfires on my part. After all, I'd already managed to shoehorn Mary Stuart into my PhD, and so I decided that yes, it was possible I might write an actual book about her, perhaps harnessing that notion of under reactivity to positive effect, plucking something publishable from one of my socially withdrawn bouts of mania for a given subject, i.e. Mary Queen of Scots. Contact was duly made with said lady from the publishing company and pretty soon I found myself putting forward an in-depth proposal for a book covering all aspects of the life of the 'tragic' Scots queen…

'V' is for…

…vaccines.

Now this is a tricky one; actually, that might be just about the biggest understatement going. Vaccines are perhaps one of the most contentious subjects within the autism community, and perhaps even the premiere debate regarding the pinpointing of the causes of autism. The main vaccine in question is the MMR vaccine – for measles, mumps and rubella – and if you Google the subject then you'll find yourself confronted with reams of fairly vitriolic back and forth between the opposing sides. Regarding my own perspective on the subject, well, mainly there was that fumbling nurse and her soft toys decoy ploy whilst administering one of my childhood jabs, but that's about it. Do I honestly think that jab gave me autism, or that it somehow triggered a slumbering gene which might otherwise have laid dormant for the rest of my life, a life where NT Me might have reigned supreme?! Who can say? I said earlier that I'm fairly certain autism isn't caused by vaccines; there are numerous people in history whom one might consider autistic and they were all around long before the various jabs that some people now seek to blame. There is, however, a certain degree of scepticism to be employed in regard to retrospective diagnoses, but that doesn't undermine them entirely. In fact, I would stick my neck out and say that I'm almost certain that vaccines don't cause autism. I have, however, learnt through experience that it's better never to quite say *never*, just in case you end up with egg all over your face several decades down the line, when some new, ground-breaking research rubbishes everything you ever believed in to begin with.

I've mentioned already that I'm not the only one with autism in my family, alongside debating the possible dubious descent from those Irish fishing communities. So, I guess what I'm trying to say is that maybe a lot of things cause autism rather than simply vaccines or else an ageing mother, which is another one I've heard bandied around the Twitter bearpit recently. And is having autism such a bad thing anyway? As I stood there in Foyles on the Charing Cross Road, looking at the displayed copies of The Little Book of Mary Queen of Scots, well, I certainly didn't think so. That's not to say that it wouldn't still have been published if I'd been neurotypical, but it was the achievement of the fact considering that I was autistic, and also considering what I'd been through with regard to my education, that really made it stand out as a pretty stunning achievement. The moment of seeing it there on the shelf in London's premiere bookstore was both overwhelming and also in a way underwhelming, because it was a moment of purely personal triumph. For those passing to and fro over my shoulder it was simply just another book on the shelves, albeit a very prettily presented one, if I do say so myself. Anyway, the point was that I had a book in the shops; I had achieved my goal in life to be a writer. I had achieved this regardless of my autism – not to mention whatever might have caused my autism in the first place – or perhaps even possibly because of my autism. This was enough, for a while.

The proposal I put forward for the Mary Queen of Scots book was accepted – after some tweaking – by the company who'd published the Jack the Ripper anthologies in which my work had also been featured. A few weeks following the thumbs-up I was given a relatively tight timeslot in which to produce some 70,000 words for publication. On top of that I also had to find various black and white illustrations for inclusion in the book and then clear them for copyright, as well as having the text proofread. That basically meant ironing out many of the long sentences I was rather fond of, alongside putting a lid – to some extent – on my propensity for alliteration.

Because my neurodiverse brain was so positively drenched in regard to Mary Queen of Scots, I managed to turn out the first 50,000 words of the book within a fortnight. After that it was something of a struggle, not to mention the fact that securing the aforementioned images was proving to be something of a logistical nightmare; I had several meltdowns and twice ended up lying on my bed with a cold flannel pressed over my eyes. I'd shunned the importance of exams as a kid – mainly because I wasn't actually at school to do them in the first place – and then later I'd relegated the possibility of finding steady employment somewhat to the shelf, and so I was determined to take this business of writing a book seriously. Eventually, besides a couple more meltdowns, I was able to send the finished manuscript off. It was sent back to me several weeks later for minor corrections and then I was left to cool my heels for a couple of months and continue with my PhD. This toing-and-froing of the manuscript was my first up-close-and-personal experience of the publishing world, and while I've sometimes scoffed at the idea that your book is your baby, that actual moment of handing the manuscript over really did feel like giving my child away into foster care or something. I was afraid that the editors might hack it to pieces, but the suggestions they made were for the most part just minor punctuation points; the content remained pretty much as was. Several more weeks passed and then I received a scan of the cover, although in the end an image of Mary Stuart more to my liking – i.e. as in personally picked by the author – was used instead.

Perhaps the biggest coup in regard to the development of the book was the fact that I managed to secure a soundbite from historical fiction writer Philippa Gregory for the front cover, a blurb then expanded upon in the opening pages. I had no 'contacts' as such in the industry and so I simply set out with my usual abundance of sass/autistic indifference to social etiquette, writing to her via the contact information on her website and simply hoping for the best. In my best neurotypical style – i.e. polite but perhaps not always to the point – I told her that I was a fledgling writer and that it would greatly fuel my career if she were to furnish me the sort of soundbite that normally sends books flying from the shelves. A few days later, one of her personal assistants got back to me and asked to be sent a copy of the book as a word document for Philippa herself to peruse. I duly sent the requested file and then sat back, keeping everything humanly possible crossed for good luck. Several more days passed before said assistant got back to me, informing me that Philippa would be pleased to provide a quote for the front cover, one which might also be used in expanded form during the opening pages. A legal document accompanied the assistant's email, cluttered with lots of vaguely intimidating jargon which I duly passed over to Steve to scrutinise, whilst I carried on with the business of being creative. My publishers were particularly pleased with me at having secured this potential sales boost, and the cover was duly reworked to include not only the quote but also the aforementioned more aesthetically pleasing image of Mary Stuart. During the whole process I found it thrilling to know that there were unseen people behind the scenes, people whom I'd never met, who were nevertheless busily helping to make this thing that I'd slaved over into something saleable, something that would see my dream of being published finally come true.

There was a long wait following on from the inclusion of the Philippa Gregory quote, during which time I continued with my PhD, sometimes still socialising with Steve's work colleagues at various City of London pubs in my spare time. I had a particular fondness for the Samuel Pepys, secreted down a little alleyway leading out toward the Thames, not far from Blackfriars and just off Upper Thames Street. There was a balcony in the back room there where you could peer out over the river and watch the police boats speeding along on some errand or other, and all of the various pleasure boats as well. When I went for these drinks, I was able to really cut loose and enjoy that office camaraderie close-up. And as I sat there sipping my 'alco-pop' and listening in on various discussions, it occurred to me that these people probably spent more time with each other than they ever did with their partners back at home. It was like they were all one big, happy extended family, and it felt for a few moments like I was living the NT Me dream I'd first begun romanticising during my days at Hackney Youth Workforce. I must have made some comment or other to this effect, because Steve soon tried to temper the way I was whitewashing an average working day at the office with a few 'harsh' truths; he tried to explain to me about office politics, for one thing, and clashing personalities and the like, but mostly it just drifted over my head. You see, I was quite drunk on the echoes of raucous laughter that accompany your average City of London liquid lunch, and the heady rush of having people to chat to who weren't for the most part swept up from the sorry fringes of society.

I remember quite distinctly the day the first copy of The Little Book of Mary Queen of Scots arrived in Steve's office, shortly before it actually hit the shelves; he and his co-workers had a chance to enthuse over it even before I did. His-then boss Andy was particularly proud, given that he had an autistic son aged seven or so, called Luke. I never met Luke, but he amused me when he once sent Andy a text asking him when he would be returning home from work, taking care to specify '…how many hours and how many minutes exactly?' before his dad would be back. Bless.

When I myself first saw the finished version of The Little Book of Mary Queen of Scots, I was mightily impressed. It was a sleek and elegant little hardback, with Philippa Gregory's quote right there directly below my own name. A couple of weeks later it went on general release, both in bookshops and also online. On that very day I met Steve after work at Broken Wharf House and we walked from there along the river, past Blackfriars and then up towards Trafalgar Square, before heading on up Charing Cross Road. Eventually we arrived at Foyles and I saw my published book right there on the shelves, for all the world to see (two copies, to boot!). I took a couple of pictures – 'shelfies' – and then we went off somewhere to have a celebratory drink. The book soared pretty high on the Amazon charts in the first few weeks but then it began fluctuating, almost from one day to the next. I became rather obsessed with checking these sales stats, until the habit got so anxiety-producing that I had to consciously rein back on how often I was doing it. Several months later I received my first royalty payments, just as I was featured in several newspapers, both local and national. There was a big piece on me in the Dundee Courier and also a smaller piece in The Scotsman; somehow, I got away with calling some of my old teachers 'sadistic' in the former, but I doubt many of them were regular subscribers to the Dundee Courier anyway. Meanwhile, friends reported seeing the book in locations as far-flung as York Minister and Penshurst Place, as well as the more 'expected' venues of Stirling Castle and also, of course,

Edinburgh Castle. I was, to say the least, pointedly proud.

Would the book have been published and out there if I hadn't had that vaccine? Well maybe it would and maybe it wouldn't; millions of people have become obsessed with Mary Queen of Scots over the years and written books about her, and I reckon that the majority of them didn't have autism. But would the book have been – to use the Philippa Gregory soundbite – '…bright and breezy', if I'd been just another of those ardent but undoubtedly neurotypical admirers? Probably not. It might instead have come into existence as just yet another po-faced, sober sort of affair, bereft of all those little quirks and verbal somersaults that characterise my frenetic approach to writing; freehand for scrawlers. No, I firmly believe that my autism helped make that book the '…bright and breezy' pleasure that it was, but where that autism actually came from is still very much open to debate. In fact, quite where the autism ends and 'I' begin is yet another one to ponder; more Rimbaud ruminations, 'I is somebody else' all over again.

So no, I don't think that a vaccine had anything to do with anyone becoming autistic, but perhaps said vaccine simply fired up some dormant neurodiverse neurons in a particular pattern, and that happens for some people and for others who become autistic it was something else entirely that 'set them off'. Or maybe not. I'm not entirely convinced either way, but I'm open to persuasion; to come at it from another angle, I am living in the 21st-century 'blame culture', after all, and thus it's always nice to have someone at whom one can point a finger at, and to berate for all of their past woes.

*

As a bit of a postscript to this chapter I'd like to point out that I didn't give out all that many copies of The Little Book of Mary Queen of Scots to friends or family. I didn't give many out because I didn't get that many author copies to begin with and I didn't have enough money to buy complimentary copies for people left, right and centre. I do remember giving a copy to Shaminder and that she was quite impressed. I was, however, quite happy to sign copies for people if they approached me; I signed one to my sister, on one of her visits from Australia, '…thanks for all your help and support', or words to that effect. But I was being sarcastic. The only thing about my sister's 'help and support' that I ever recalled was her sniggering at me whilst being driven in our dad's car, with her saying, 'You've got to go to school tomorrow!' – this on the way back from a visit to the Maudsley hospital, where doctors had decreed that the residents of Ravensbourne Boys School were quite justified in their responses to my 'belligerence'. Later on, she had 'cause' to snigger again when a neighbour asked how I was getting on at senior school; apparently the fact that I'd been expelled and was currently between schools was enough to warrant another one of her snide little guffaws. Still, I wish her well, currently clinging on to her twenty-seventh boyfriend, or whatever; I lost count around the early 90s.

My mum was rather more charitable about my hardships and therefore the message I wrote in her copy of the book was entirely sincere; she now keeps it on permanent display on a shelf in the living room. Several of my relatives have brought copies as well, but as I don't see most of them from one year to the next, it's hard to pinpoint who supported me with their goodwill and their wallet and who didn't. I think I should make a special mention of my Auntie Joyce, though, who was delighted to be able to call her nephew an author, proudly showing the book to all of her friends and neighbours and even to the postman, so I'm told.

'W' is for…

…wildlife.

Now I've spoken before about my many beloved cats, about Anna and Julie and Emma, Sam and Wolvie and Tiggy, and so on and so forth. When I was little, I also had a rabbit and a guinea pig called Snowball and Bobbity respectively; they lived in a hutch outside and when Bobbity eventually died, Snowball pined and then died herself within a couple of days. We never had a dog, although my dad loved dogs. Auntie Joyce always had dogs and I liked visiting them because when I was young I used to eat the dog biscuits, mainly because they looked like miniature Jammie Dodgers and eating dog biscuits is one of the less peculiar things an autistic child might try out from time to time. I also had – but not ate, I must stress – a few goldfish over the years, but these were always the pitiful specimens won as fairground prizes and which used to expire the morning after you'd brought them home. I also remember taking in a stray caterpillar from the garden when I was really small and making a home for it in a transparent Tupperware box, with a little bed made out of folded toilet paper. The caterpillar was one of those black and orange ones that used to move around like a Slinky toy, leaving a trail of little green droppings in its wake. I was really quite distraught when it died, failing in its predestined future – as I was led to believe – of curling up into a chrysalis and then re-emerging as a beautiful butterfly.

Apparently, having an affinity with animals is something I share with a great many autistic people. It's also something that has been widely recognised of late by those pioneering various ways to 'alleviate' the day to day difficulties of autistic people. Several news stories in recent times have covered the charming relationships between autistic children and their pets; always a kid, mind you, because no one seems to want to see a forty-something autistic man fawning over his golden retriever. Apparently, you can also now have an 'autism assistance dog' if you so require. A quick peek at the website for 'autism assistance dogs' revealed the rather non-shocking fact that their 'assistance dogs' are purely for children; once again adults with autism are rendered largely invisible, as though autism were some sort of childhood malady that miraculously evaporates by the time a person turns eighteen or so.

On this basis – I could also cite countless twee tales on Twitter of 'aspie' kids and their kittens – it does seem that people with autism really do have a certain special affinity for animals. Unfortunately, there is also a flipside to this charming relationship between the species, of caring too much for our sweet and cuddly friends. For me it began during my early twenties, viewing some particularly unpalatable animal cruelty footage on 'The James Whale Show', transmitted late at night on a Friday evening. It stuck with me for years – to this very day even – these various grainy vignettes, one of which showed a man kicking and beating a pig across a sullen concrete farmyard. The worst of all was the footage of the three men digging up a fox in a darkened wood and holding the screaming creature up to the camera before they did god only knows what to the poor little thing. Like I said, the images stuck with me to this day, but they never held such sway that I attempted to change my lifestyle in any significant way, shape or form. Fast-forward twelve years or so and then I did make the choice to cut pork and all pig-related products from my diet. This happened when I saw an item on the national news about abuse at an abattoir somewhere in the Midlands. I'd choked on a bit of bacon when I was a kid so cutting that out proved no real problem, given that autistic people tend to have very long memories when it comes to being slighted, intentionally or otherwise. I still miss ham somewhat, though. However, vegan sausages are so good these days that you can barely taste the difference. The point is, clearly something was shifting in my psyche.

Every year I would make it one of my New Year's resolutions to try and do something to alleviate animal cruelty a little; one year I volunteered for the Cats Protection League, although they never actually bothered getting back to me. They wanted my money, but they didn't want my time offered as a useful volunteer. I tucked that rebuff into my back pocket and started scouring around on Facebook, to see what else I could do to help my fellow earthlings, and from there I rapidly came across that movie.

'Earthlings' is a 2005 documentary film directed by Shaun Monson, with narration by actor Joaquin 'Joker' Phoenix, and with a haunting score by Moby. The Wikipedia page describes it simply as '…a 2005 American documentary film about humanity's use of other animals as pets, food, clothing, entertainment, and for scientific research.' It is also 95 minutes of sheer, unrelenting animal cruelty. I read countless accounts of how harrowing the film was and even watched some YouTube videos where people actually filmed themselves reacting it; you could hear what was going on in the film but you couldn't actually see anything because the camera was pointing at the person watching it. Numerous people online referred to the movie as 'the vegan-maker', attesting to its power and its potency, whereby shell-shocked viewers would swear off meat and all other animal-related products almost overnight. For several months I skirted around various websites praising the film, 'liking' on Facebook a host of pages devoted to exposing animal cruelty of all sorts; the 'League Against Cruel Sports' and other similar organisations, for instance. With hindsight I might have been better off simply gouging out my soul with a rusty spoon. You see, my autistically obsessive nature latched onto the subject of animal cruelty in almost exactly the same way it had devoured Anne Boleyn and Mary Queen of Scots, Rimbaud and the various fictional worlds of Anne Rice. But this, like health anxiety, was a negative obsession, albeit one with highly honourable intentions. Basically, my neurodiverse brain had grabbed and then gorged on a series of horrid statistics in much the same way as it had cleverly assimilated every significant date concerned with Anne Boleyn's meteoric rise to power. Horrific images were searing themselves onto my psyche with alarming regularity; I ended up having to 'unlike' most, if not all, of those Facebook pages to whom I'd wanted to show support. However, there were times when it felt like it was too late and that the damage to my delicate neural pathways had already been done.

I never actually watched 'Earthlings', though, and I probably never will. For me the reasoning behind this rather rigid stance stems from that old saying about '…the best swords staying firmly in their scabbards', or some such. In other words, it's so awful that simply knowing about it is enough; you don't have to put yourself through the wringer by actually watching the thing. I found it on YouTube once during the early days of my exploration into the subject and I actually started to watch it; I must have lasted maybe ninety seconds before I was forced to turn off. I got past the poignant, haunting opening titles relatively unscathed, the camerawork involving some spectacular panoramic shots of the planet; indeed, it was the sort of stuff you might see in the first few seconds of any decent sci-fi movie. Moby's music was particularly pained, though; one might even call it 'hopeless'. Then a caption filled the screen which read 'earth-ling *noun*. One who inhabits the earth.' Joaquin Phoenix then explained the term over various shots of humanity, of fishes in the sea, dogs and lion cubs playing, lobsters, birds, reptiles, frogs, fishes and so on and so forth, and then the grainy black and white footage/animal cruelty began. I lasted maybe ten seconds from that point, peering from behind my fingers at some aerial view of a Spanish bull-run, watching a group of people tugging the poor, reluctant creature along a busy street by means of a large rope. I tried jumping forwards in the narrative somewhat, this time finding myself confronted with what looked like – and here I only lasted a mere fraction of a second – a whale, still alive, being driven along on the back of a big lorry, tethered down by a large, leathery harness. I knew it was still alive because it was writhing, and its tail was flopping limply from side to side. Those brief glimpses of brutality only confirmed for me the idea that this film was so potent that the mere legend of it might be enough to kick-start the conscience of the most ardent carnivore. I myself gave up meat later that year, making a big deal of consuming my last ever KFC, gobbling down as much of the greasy stuff as I could before I became firstly a vegetarian and then finally a full-blown vegan.

Becoming a vegetarian was relatively easy; meat substitutes are now so good – as I said – that I barely missed meat at all, although there's no point denying that I loved the taste of KFC and always will, but you'll find plenty of vegetarians/vegans who will readily admit to something akin. However, I found myself faced with a far greater challenge when it came to cutting out dairy products. Where dairy cruelty was concerned I could claim total ignorance; it really had never occurred to me that a cow had to be pregnant to make milk, and to make the amount of milk consumed daily across the country, that most cows would need to be almost continually pregnant. They don't get any say in the matter, of course, forcibly impregnated repeatedly until their wombs are literally worn out. I set out looking for a milk substitute, working my way through almost all of the dairy alternatives, from soy milk to hemp milk to coconut milk (which gave me terrible cramps) before finally settling on almond milk. Now it's not perfect by any means but it comes the closest to dairy and it only leaves me feeling a little bit bloated when consumed in large amounts, i.e. over my morning bowl of Frosties. Vegan cheese substitutes were a little more trial and error, and a couple of them were – if I'm being completely honest – a little rancid and rubbery. I also miss a lot of my favourite yogurts now and I'm still making the odd mistake and eating something dessert-ish that actually has dairy in it, but it's all about intent. I have to say that because a lot of vegans are very militant about the whole movement, which is fair enough when you actually see what the animals have to go through, but sometimes they can be so judgemental that they almost make you want to go and have a KFC just to spite them.

I was also totally ignorant about sweets and the whole gelatine issue; what a sad day it was when I waved farewell to so many of my favourite Haribo treats, especially the super sour Haribo 'Tangtastics'. Thankfully Marks & Spencer positively shine with their range of veggie and vegan sweets, including several members of the cherished 'Percy Pig' range.

Later on, during that first initial foray into veganism, I made an attempt – and the key word here is 'attempt' – to attend my first ever animal rights protest/rally. This was an event staged regularly right in the middle of Piccadilly Circus, put together by a group of rather hard-line vegans. At these events they give out leaflets and offer friendly advice, the whole thing punctuated by loudspeakers carrying audio footage from the 'Earthlings' movie; that or else some 'unusual' songs about various aspects of the animal liberation movement. For maybe half an hour or more I lingered on the fringes of this little scene, until one of the activists spotted me and then duly dragged me over. I think I told him on the spot that I was autistic, therefore excusing my poor eye contact and also my somewhat spontaneous conversational shifts. Following on from him, a rather stunning Romanian woman called Helena stepped forward and really talked me through the whole business; as I listened, I was distinctly struck by what appeared to be an awful sadness behind her eyes. I call her my 'vegan godmother' now, and I'm still quite convinced that the sadness I saw came from the fact that she'd probably seen 'Earthlings' all the way through. My initial enthusiasm won me a place behind their little stall handing out leaflets and even wearing one of those infamous 'Meat is murder' t-shirts; the fallout exploded on Facebook later that day when it became clear that I was actually only – at that point – a budding vegan. Cue my first experience of the dark side of the vegan crusade, and the reason so many people seem to hold them in such low esteem. As a result of my autistic honesty in regard to how rapidly I was 'transitioning', a veritable war of words erupted online, regarding whose decision it had been to allow me to man the stall when I wasn't yet a fully-fledged vegan. I took a step back and kept well out of it, but I'd had my fingers well and truly burned, and it would be several long months before I next dipped my toe into the fraught world of real-life activism; hello Canada Goose on Regent Street. In the meantime, I explored other avenues of protest and direct action, including attending an outreach hosted at the Lush 'fresh handmade cosmetics' shop in Victoria Station, thrown by a bunch of hunt saboteurs. I was on board for about a minute, until one of them explained to me the hard logistics of getting up at the crack of dawn so that you can be driven down to a misty, dewy field in the middle of nowhere, with the quite distinct possibility that the pro-hunt supporters will physically attack you for your efforts. I took away a 'brochure' and spent the train journey home reading the obituary of a man who'd died on just such a 'sab' after being set upon by those aforementioned pro-hunt supporters. I wasn't even home before I decided that life as a saboteur wasn't for me and that maybe the protests at Piccadilly were in fact the softer way to put my feelings into action, judgemental Facebook misunderstandings aside.

By the time I eventually re-joined the Piccadilly protestors I was a fully-fledged vegan. As it turned out they weren't really keeping score, because several months had since elapsed and the man who'd made the most fuss on Facebook didn't seem to be hanging around anymore. Now at this point you might be wondering how someone with autism might stand there in the middle of Piccadilly Circus on a Saturday lunchtime and hand out flyers on such a contentious issue to members of the general public, amidst all that noise and bustle. The fact is, I found that the plight of the animals gave me 'a voice' in the same way that the simple companionship of all of my various cats gave me – and other autistics – something a bit beyond the usual pet/owner relationship. Initially I simply handed out the flyers, meekly moving to left and right to avoid the stream of people passing the stall, most of whom tended to wrinkle their noses when they saw what we were all about. However, after a couple of weeks I found that I was actually talking to these people, engaging with them, 'working the pavement' and sometimes even prancing to and fro between one passer-by and another in my desire to spread the vegan message. I had become a bit like one of those missionaries who walks along the road chanting and beating the tambourine. I'm not entirely sure if it made for much of an edifying sight, but it certainly felt good; it felt emboldening, more to the point, and that is a very powerful feeling for a normally rather introverted autistic person. After the 'outreach', most of my fellow protestors would head on into Soho and to the 'Vegan Hippo' café/restaurant. Unfortunately, the place was barely big enough to swing a cat in – if you'll pardon the topical pun – and so I ended up sitting cheek to jowl with my fellow diners, with no wide pavements to cavort around upon and so I became your classic autistic again, resplendent with communication problems and various eye contact issues.

I've since heard several people liken being a vegan in 2017 to what it must have been like being gay in the late 1980s; progress is being made, very clearly, but most people still despise you and also there's pretty much nowhere decent to hang out. Still, it feels sort of fun, being in on the ground floor of a social movement and all. I've pretty much converted Steve, but I had some 'help' in that department courtesy of his irritable bowel syndrome and all the things he had to give up eating as a result. His niece Gemma is a veggie as well and I'm hoping that given time – and some rather unsubtle hints from me – she might make the switch to vegan proper. She doesn't say much, but like me she loves her wildlife, and so I think in that case perhaps few words are needed after all.

'X' is for...

...X, Fragile, otherwise known as Fragile X syndrome.

For this one I'll start by reiterating the fact that the internet is a boon to people like me, an autistic adult who finds social interaction somewhat stressful at the best of times. Facebook has been fantastic when it comes to setting up safe spaces to interact with people, and Twitter has also been great for promoting my crusade regarding the fact that autism isn't 'just' a childhood 'affliction', but instead a lifelong condition. But there's a dark side to the internet too; I'm not talking about the so-called 'dark web' here, but merely the fact of having all that information at your fingertips, especially when you're somewhat soft-hearted and credulous by nature. Thus, it was that when first I began Googling various topics related to autism I also came upon a heap of other things – related – that I'd never even considered before. These discoveries soon struck me dumb with terror because I thought that I might 'have' them as well, simply because I was autistic. And that brings me rather neatly to the somewhat sinister sounding Fragile X syndrome, which sounds a bit like something out of a Marvel Comics movie, and in any other circumstance that might be just cool, but clearly here it isn't.

Fragile X syndrome is a cellular mutation which can be linked to some cases of autism. Unlike autism, Fragile X Syndrome also has some marked physical characteristics, including a long face and noticeably large ears. As far as I'm aware I have neither of those traits, but this didn't stop me fretting that I was in fact carrying these mutated Fragile X syndrome genes, which might somehow spontaneously manifest when I was least expecting it. I sent out discreet enquiries on Twitter and even considered delving into my family's medical history in some detail, but I drew back in the end, afraid of what other lurking genetic skeletons I might uncover. The non-physical symptoms of Fragile X syndrome tallied so closely with the standard traits of autism that I continued to remain overwrought for quite some time. I think maybe my whole health anxiety disorder stepped in at this point and had a hand in upping the general angst level. Eventually I was forced to make a vow never to research the 'medical' side of autism online again, lest I stumble across some other condition which might in some way be linked to autism by a few dangling strands of particularly pernicious DNA. This was a salutary lesson in not simply sitting there and Googling just because you have all of that unfiltered knowledge at your fingertips; knowledge is power, yes, but ignorance is bliss. I think on reflection I'd rather be happily ignorant as opposed to powerfully neurotic.

During my searches I also happened upon a great deal of online literature informing me of the fact that most autistic adults ended up dead before they reached the age of forty, or else shortly thereafter. This sent me into a panic akin to the discovery of the Fragile X syndrome; I imagined my neurodiverse DNA gradually unravelling until I literally dissolved into a puddle, somewhere just shy of my fortieth birthday party. Further perusal of said articles informed me of the fact that this spike in deaths was actually caused by large numbers of autistic adults taking their own lives; in fact, one article said that they were nine times more likely to try and take their own life compared to your average neurotypical person. The National Autistic Society were on record remarking what an outrage the whole thing was, urging the NHS to carry out more research into this 'shocking' statistic; a Swedish study confirmed that the average age of death for an autistic person was fifty-four, male or female. I wondered whether or not the sporadic inability to concentrate coherently was a factor – i.e. mown down simply whilst crossing the road – but far more likely, I figured, these people were dying simply because they were lonely and isolated. I might have told the researchers that possibly another of the main reasons for all these suicides might have been the near – if you'll pardon the irony – autistic-level obsession with focusing entirely on children with autism, literally to the exclusion of all else. Kids with autism are at odds with their environment but at that age the behavioural excesses can be reconfigured into something quirky or cute; when you see an adult displaying those behaviours then most people just call it '...downright weird.' Of course, there are those poor kids on the harsher end of 'the spectrum', those whose outbursts of violence and public meltdowns are anything but cute; I saw some of them on a Louis Theroux documentary I watched the other day. Louis Theroux interviewed a bunch of kids and their families over in America, kids who were speeding towards puberty and rapidly outsizing their poor, helpless parents in the process; one mother was forced to lie on top of her son on a crashmat whenever he exhibited a particularly boisterous 'behaviour'. Still, despite all of their trials they had a huge, state-of-the-art school to attend. In the same vein, when I talked to Steve's old boss Andy about how his little Luke was getting on, I found out that he gets ferried to school in a taxi! A taxi!! – things had clearly moved on greatly from the days when I was ferried to Foxley special needs school in the dreaded 'spag wagon', but I'm not bitter about the mod-cons today's autistic kids have access to. Well, not much, anyway.

*

Cate, the lady who'd commissioned my Little Book of Mary Queen of Scots, left the publishing company responsible for producing that rather sublime tome and took it upon herself to set up her own fledgling enterprise. A few weeks later she sent me an email, offering me a three-book contract to produce a series of Tudor tomes to be published over the next couple of years. I don't have to tell you that I almost bit off her hand in accepting this honour; to see another book with my name on it upon those hallowed Foyles shelves seemed almost too wonderful a prospect to articulate.

Over the next few weeks she sent me a series of blueprints on which I should base her three separate ideas. The contract stipulated that I was to write all three books pretty much back to back but that it would then take several years for all of them to actually see print. The first was to be a gift book, in full colour, called 'I Love the Tudors'. I actually wanted it to be called 'Tudor Titbits' but that suggestion sort of got lost in the various emails sent back and forth over the following few months. Eventually I rather took to the new title and part of that process was realising that other points of view besides my own autistic tunnel-vision existed, and that there were some subjects on which other people were actually more knowledgeable than I myself was.

I wrote most of that first book at Steve's new flat in Cheam Village, spending days with my notes and also with as many Tudor books as I could muster, all spread out on a big glass table in front of me, the sun streaming through a pair of big bay windows to my right. I drank endless cups of tea and consumed vast amounts of Marks and Spencer

'Percy Pigs' as I toiled away. I even enlisted my 'Doctor Who' friend Neil to come over on several occasions, specifically when my inspiration dried up and I was running short of facts for pages as-yet filled. Unlike The Little Book of Mary Queen of Scots, 'I Love the Tudors' was to feature wholly new illustrations rather than those already in existence in the public domain; Cate herself would take care of all that, so I didn't need to worry about any bothersome copyright business. Instead I could concern myself purely with the task of writing the thing.

At around this time, my obsessions were also still wrestling with the awful reality of the whole animal rights thing, as much as they were also still concerned with the minutiae of Anne Boleyn's daily life. Just like the fact that one's nicer autistic obsessions never really leave, so it is that you never seem quite able to shake the nastier notions in the back of your mind either. Thankfully the writing of the new Tudor book managed to prove itself enough of a pleasant distraction that I didn't find myself subtly overwhelmed with a cacophony of unpleasant animal cruelty images. In order to distance my mind still further from this possibility, I began dipping my toe into the whole business of mindfulness, reading this or that webpage and so on and so forth, climbing onto the back of what was already by then a fairly well-established movement/fad. Fast-forward several years and I'm still practicing mindfulness and finding that it really can help soften some of the harsher autistic symptoms. I recently read some stuff by Ruby Wax, and I find her voice on the subject really fits in with how I like to manage my own approach to mindfulness. If they taught autistic people how to manage their symptoms by using mindfulness, well then, I reckon they might really be able to slash that dreadful suicide rate.

I sent the finished manuscript for what would eventually become 'I Love the Tudor's off to Cate and then took several months out to concentrate on polishing up my PhD. This was still proving rather problematic, as I couldn't grasp the simple fundamentals of writing a properly considered/academically rigorous analysis chapter. On that basis I had another extensive solo tutorial with Jenny Owen and over the space of some three hours we managed to hammer out a fairly decent strategy for me to try and complete the analysis chapter before yet another year passed; the dream of actually completing the thing full-time was long since dashed and I was now basically working to a part-time action plan. A couple of weeks after sending the 'I Love the Tudors' manuscript to Cate, I submitted what I hoped would be my finished thesis to my tutors, to peruse 'at their leisure'.

'I Love the Tudors' was released in January of 2016, to a modest fanfare; a few more newspaper articles and a brief but pointed spell at the top of the Amazon book charts, in the Tudor subsection. I dedicated the book to my tutors Shaminder and Jenny because of their endless patience in steering me a path through my PhD; I think they were very pleased to receive their signed copies. I sent a couple more copies off to various friends around the country but I couldn't bring myself to have a book launch or even to do a proper book signing; the prospect of speaking aloud before a large group of people or even meeting the public in any significant numbers still turned me into a shivering wreck; maybe I'll try it with the next one.

As with The Little Book of Mary Queen of Scots, I enjoyed hearing from various people that they had seen 'I Love the Tudors' in different historical locations scattered around the country; like the former, it was spotted in York Minster and Penshurst Place, as well as Ludlow Castle, to name just a few. I myself was of course happy enough simply to see several copies available on the Tudor specified shelf at Foyles, with a few friends spying it there and sending me selfies in which they were waving one of the copies around in a state of frenzied delight.

In the wake of this latest success, I experienced feelings similar to those that had percolated around my mind when The Little Book of Mary Queen of Scots first hit the shelves. Basically, I envisioned myself walking into one of my old schools and promptly slapping one of my books down upon the reception desk, declaring to all and sundry, 'There! Despite your best efforts I managed to write that!'. I doubt I would ever actually go that far, though; I mean, I know that revenge is a dish best served cold, but do I really want to come across like I've been waiting some forty-odd years to serve it up?!? No, but I do quite fancy the idea of somehow showing them that, despite their disdain, I still managed to see my dreams of a published book come true. Of course, I'm also quite well aware of the fact that 'them', like myself, are now long since grownup and perhaps gone off who knows where, but that's the beauty of the internet, I suppose; you can pinpoint practically anyone, no matter how far back they featured in your life. However, a far nobler daydream might instead be to use my example – my whole sorry life story, really – to show those autistic kids growing up today that even if you don't get a half-decent start in life – a half-decent education – that you can still see your dreams coming true before your very eyes, if you just hold on and persevere.

'Y' is for…

…Y-Chromosome.

The 'Y-Chromosome' theory introduces the idea that people with autism are actually affected by a mutation in their genes, specifically something to do with the Y-Chromosome. The Y-Chromosome determines the sex, not only in humans but in many other species; a mutation concerning the Y-Chromosome might be the reason that some people are autistic, although let me stress again that this is merely a theory. To the best of my knowledge it is still one of the more prominent ideas concerning the origins of autism. For me it was the word 'mutation' that appealed, mainly because for several decades I've been an ardent fan of Marvel Comics' 'X-Men' series. The X-Men are a group of people born with strange and uncanny powers, often ostracised and hunted down by society and the government as a result, all whilst busily saving a world that '…fears and hates them.' I have a couple of X-Men tattoos, several of which I still adore but one of which I really rather regret. When I was hanging around with Nicky Crane, I was stupid enough to get both my hands covered in tattoos – your bog-standard cobweb and also a few childish phrases – courtesy of a tattooist in Notting Hill Gate who hung around in the same circles as the aforementioned Mr Crane. I think his name was Marc Saint, actually, and I'm sure his studio was somewhere on the Portobello Road. As far as I also recall, having one's hands tattooed was illegal, either that or I think you had to be over twenty-one or something in order to make that rather rash judgement call, but despite all that, this guy unleashed his ink on me and my sometimes questionable autistic judgement did the rest. Several years later my parents kindly paid for me to have the tattoos on my hands removed at a posh Harley Street clinic. I can tell you that having tattoos removed is way worse than having them done in the first place. Firstly, one dons a pair of protective goggles, before a laser is blasted into the ink with the most appalling banging sound going on in the background, rather like an Ack-ack gun being fired. The skin then blisters and boils and swells under the onslaught of the laser. I would then leave the tattoo removal clinic with both hands wrapped in bandages, through which blood and pus were quite often clearly seen to be seeping; from that point it would take several days for the swelling and the stinging to subside. At that point a special balm was then to be administered at least once a day, in order to facilitate further disintegration of the tattoo inks. Now, several years later, I no longer have any tattoos on my hands reminding me how foolish I once was, apart from the ghost image of one particular symbol that stubbornly refused to submit to the rigorous attentions of the laser. That blurred remnant stands as a sobering reminder of just how bad that judgement of mine really was back before I got a handle on my autistic mind-set.

The first person to bring my attention to the whole 'Y-Chromosome' thing was a young guy taking my picture at the Tower of London, on a bright but slightly breezy day back in April 2016. This guy wasn't just randomly taking my picture, though (I'm marginally photogenic); I was there for a photoshoot for my university – London South Bank – to showcase students who had achieved something a little out of the ordinary during the course of their studies. The fact that I'd had several books published after being kicked out of school at the age of twelve, not to mention my four degrees and my PhD looming, qualified me as a potential subject to be placed before the lens. Two guys from the university turned up that day, one of them the photographer and the other the actual guy organising the initiative on the university's behalf. The idea was that pictures would be taken of chosen subjects – i.e. me – and then blown up into giant canvases that would adorn the entrance halls of some of the university buildings; several other students were also involved, although I was basically only interested in the fact that I'd been selected for this singular honour; autistic bubble, and all that. About a year later the exercise would be repeated in roughly the same fashion, except then it was a prose article that would appear in the LSBU prospectus for the new academic year – more on that later.

As part of the photoshoot I was told to pose with both of my books – The Little Book of Mary Queen of Scots/I Love the Tudors respectively – with the Tower of London providing a topical backdrop to the whole thing. While we were busy trying out various angles, the young guy with the camera began quizzing me on what else it was I'd done that was so very 'special'. Besides the books, I rapidly listed my numerous degrees, alongside my autistically arduous battle through the education system, to which he then replied, 'Autism…isn't that caused by some sort of mutation with the 'Y' bits of your DNA or something?!', eyeing me curiously in the speckled midday sun, like I really did look like one of the freakier members of the X-Men or something.

I had to confess to him that I'd never heard of the

possibility of 'mutation' before, at least not where the various possible causes of autism were concerned. I put both of my books down and then I told him all about childhood vaccines and also about the many hereditary and genetic elements also possibly involved. I then confessed that the possibility of 'mutations' was new to me, but also that it sounded rather exciting, in a vaguely childlike/comic book kind of a way. Over the course of the photoshoot it became clear that this young photographer knew far more about the subject than I did, further explaining to me his idea that the 'Y-Chromosome' theory was also linked to issues of a hereditary nature, alongside that idea of cells mutating. I can't emphasise enough how much I embraced that word 'mutating' and how much I liked the idea that it hinted at people with autism 'unmasked' as a race of mutants, perhaps in fact a whole new strand of humanity altogether. It was a slight but satisfying variation on the idea of autistic people as 'children of the gods', as voiced by that dreadful gum-chewing American woman in my creative writing class, several years previously; I imagined her honking in protest at this proposal against her rather more dour ideas on the subject.

The photoshoot took several hours and in some ways it was perhaps one of the proudest moments of my life, but it was also occasionally rather excruciating. Of course people stared, wondering why I was having my picture taken in the first place and whether or not I was in fact some sort of Z-list celebrity; a girl sprawling around the concourse was asked to move by my esteemed photographer; she slowly turned around, taking in the humble spectacle of myself, her eyes drifting up and down before she sort of shrugged and then went off on her way. There was nothing nasty about it, but I guess she just wondered who the hell I was that I could be the one to gouge her out of her chosen little spot like that.

Sometimes the photographer told me to smile and to

hold the books up in what seemed a vaguely cheesy fashion, and at other times he told me to look as though I were reading them intently, and having a thoroughly good time in the process; that dual emotion was pretty hard to convey with my vaguely static bog-standard autistic expression. However, the finished pictures were actually pretty good, handy when it came to constructing my website, where they were employed as publicity shots, although they were in such hi-res that you could see every little line, wrinkle and spot upon my face; some touching up was required before I allowed them to enter the public domain.

As we were finishing up for the day, I managed to catch a couple more snippets from the photographer guy concerning his various autism theories; he told me about how the whole 'Y-Chromosome' theory also indicated that many more men than women appeared to have autism. Now that wasn't the first time I'd heard this idea, but recently there has been a commendable upsurge – especially on Twitter – of women with autism making their voices heard. I think it was at this point that I began to feel a little uncomfortable with all of this talk of causes and extra genes and the like – the marvellous 'mutation' word aside – because the conversation seemed bound to drift at some point towards the question of 'cures'. In fact, several of the larger autism charities have come under fire because their dogma seems directed more to 'curing' autism than to helping people manage the condition on a day-to-day basis; never mind the fact that some of the world's most talented innovators also happen to have autism and where would we be without them. I guess this whole line of thinking drifts towards eugenics and Nazis and of course a delicious dollop of irony, if you consider the possible political leanings of the late 'great' Dr Asperger.

I met up with Steve during the photoshoot at the Tower of London and when I was done posing, I walked with him into the City and we had lunch at a bar near to the Monument. Over my vegan lunch I asked him what he thought I should do if one day someone came up with a 'cure' for autism. As I said it, I imagined this cure like some glistening substance secreted in a small phial, with the words 'Drink me' written in swirling Italics on the cork at the top. Steve absolutely baulked at the suggestion that I should take such a thing and change who I was, although I couldn't help but remember the semi-tragic character of 'Rogue', perhaps one of my favourite members of the X-Men. Rogue could absorb anyone's powers and personality simply by touching her skin to theirs; it only lasted about an hour, but the lamentable point was that she couldn't turn this power off and whoever she touched – accidentally or otherwise – went into a temporary coma until the effects had worn off. She therefore went about clothed from head to toe in a black body-stocking – with a torn green vest on top to make it look a little snazzier – and couldn't even hug someone in case she accidentally touched them and thus knocked them out. In the third movie of the X-Men franchise, a potential cure for mutants and their powers is developed and Rogue goes off at once to seek said cure and be turned into a 'normal' person; as she'd probably never been laid I could sort of see where she was coming from. One of the other X-Men tried to point out that she didn't need a cure because there was nothing wrong with her, but it didn't hold much water as far as I was concerned. I'd always felt a certain sort of doom-laden affinity with Rogue, but I don't think I actually wanted to be her.

As I gazed around that bustling City bar, in the wake of having downed this imaginary cure, the spectre of NT Me shimmered and then solidified amongst the crowds of carefree young office workers. I marvelled as he held his own amidst their rapid-fire banter, and with considerable neurotypical aplomb at that. The fantasy really unfurled as I imagined him walking out of that bar without a single person turning their gaze towards his gait, everything he'd said well measured and considered, without any sudden deviations in tone or topic, or any outright interruptions. And off he went into the sunset and lived happily ever after.

It's risking the opprobrium of the neurodiverse community to admit to being at least a bit tempted by the prospect of a 'cure', but for the most part I'd like to think that I was by then – circa 2016 – actually fairly settled into my autistic identity. Okay, so sometimes it's hard to know where Mickey ends and the autism begins, or indeed vice versa, but I'm so used to it now that I think I'd be like a fish out of water if someone were to suddenly zap me 'normal'; as I said, maybe Rogue just wasn't quite as risqué as I used to think, after all.

It was around this time, with the help of social media platforms like Facebook and Twitter, that I declared my neurodiversity to the world – or basically anyone who could be bothered to follow me – whilst at the same time using the relative anonymity of the laptop to shield me from the judgements of said world if and when they came. And so, whilst the whole 'Y-Chromosome' thing really did sound like something out of the X-Men, it was in a sense almost as bothersome as the whole Fragile X syndrome, and likewise best left well enough alone. For me the lesson I'd learnt during that photoshoot was that the more medical side of neurodiversity was perhaps rightly reserved for the experts, whilst I myself should maybe appreciate more the ways in which being autistic had enriched my life, rather than constantly yearning for the simple fact of being able to walk in a straight line unimpeded.

'Z' is for…

…zoning out.

…or perhaps – and more in keeping with the intentionally inspirational tone of the book – going from 'zero' to 'hero'. Anyway. I find myself zoning out more and more these days, basically just switching off, and this is most definitely a result of feeling more comfortable with my neurodiversity, especially in public places. Sometimes it comes as the result of simply too much sensory overload; say I'm walking down a busy street and I've got faces flying at me in all directions, and there comes a point where I simply can't process all of the enhanced sights and sounds anymore. At that point I just take myself to one side – a shop doorway is always handy – and I simply stand there and switch off until I feel ready to go 'online' again; I zone out, in other words. You could relate this process to turning your mobile phone onto the 'airplane' setting, so that basically everything essential is still functioning but nothing else is going to get through. You might think of zoning out as the antithesis of mindfulness, because whereas with mindfulness you pay the utmost attention to the present moment and enjoy the minutiae of everyday life, with zoning out it's the exact opposite; you're so overloaded with stimuli that you simply have to switch to autopilot in order to maintain your sanity. Perhaps instead of the 'airplane' setting, imagine that it's like the volume control on a remote; for an autistic person, this particular control doesn't respond when they try turning it down, and so zoning out is the only way to regain one's equilibrium. We all need a little escape valve now and then, and for me at least zoning out is a pretty foolproof way to escape from a rather overactive, excitable world.

I zoned out soon after I found out that my Little Book of Mary Queen of Scots was going to a second printing. Everyone was so excited on my behalf that some serious back-slapping and hearty congratulations ensued – any excuse for a drink and all that – and eventually I had to excuse myself and scamper upstairs to my room, slamming the door behind me and arranging myself on my bed in a vaguely corpse-like fashion, hands folded calmly across my chest. I then closed my eyes, content simply to follow those strange, pulsing colours that undulate behind your eyelids when you've got them closed but when you're actually still wide awake. Gradually the sound of downstairs drifted away into a low hum and then the sounds outside my window melted away into just the occasional birdcall, and little else besides.

These days I'm actually finding that the more things are going my way the less I'm wanting to partake in the sorts of social swirls NT Me might have enjoyed; perhaps now, at this point in my life, it might even be worth parking the ambition of NT Me once and for all. It's unlikely – although not impossible, and I still harbour it as a secret fantasy – that I'll ever land myself a regular job in a regular office in the City of London, taking liquid lunches with my workmates and becoming involved in the more pleasing aspects of office politics. Over the years I've worked in a Dunkin' Doughnuts, in a gym, in a nightclub, as a nightclub leafleter on the streets of Soho; as a film reviewer and now currently as a writer and researcher, but still I can't quite quash that hankering for a normal nine-to-five occupation, with the required commute and all of the other stuff that goes along with it. But for now I'll have to content myself with continuing to live vicariously through the details of Steve's daily grind, pointing out how lucky he is to be surrounded by people from nine in the morning until five in the evening, whereas I'm left sitting in the gilded cage that is my room, tapping away on my keyboard and hoping fervently that the world takes notice. Having said that, I do have an appointment forthcoming with a company that specialises in training up autistic adults for interviews and equipping them with the skills they'll need to survive your average modern job interview. Maybe I'll get that job in the City after all, even if it's just a bit of simple admin or something; heck, I'd even be satisfied wheeling the tea trolley around the place.

Soon after the confirmation of a second print-run for the Little Book of Mary Queen of Scots, I was contacted once more by the marketing office of London South Bank University; they asked if I would like to participate in a case study to be used in the university's promotional material, most likely for the forthcoming academic year. This was somewhat like the recent photoshoot at the Tower of London, although this time around the thing would take the form of an article which would be posted onto the university's website as a sort of 'success story', used to lure in prospective new students. I was sent a form by a marketing firm who specialised in arranging these sorts of things, which I dutifully filled in and then sent back; a week or so later I was sent a rough draft of what the finished thing would look like. I scanned it, gave it the thumbs-up and then off it went. Then it was time to sit back and enjoy the fact that my academic path was now being used as a positive example for others to follow, a hearty achievement considering that – forgive me, but I simply love repeating it – I'd actually left mainstream school aged twelve and then spent my early teens locked up at home under a form of house arrest. I like to think that this example of positive affirmation is quite an accolade, and that it ties in nicely with the overall theme of this little autobiography, a tale of the disadvantaged disabled triumphing over nit-picking prejudice. Basically put, I was going to have my education and become a writer no matter how much school I missed out on and no matter what other people did to me in the process. I also thought that my story might serve as a sort of cautionary horror tale about how badly an individual life can derail when the education system lets you down. There's no point polishing everything with that sheen of positive affirmation; I made some serious errors of judgement during my misspent youth, and I often wonder how things might have turned out had I 'toughed it out' at Ravensbourne Boys School, sticking around to see where a relatively stable education might have taken me. I doubt that things would likely have turned out that much differently; in fact, they may have gotten much worse and I might have had more tales of trauma and abuse with which to furnish the first few chapters of this book. Anyway, most likely I would have ended up being expelled anyway; I still don't think that glancing at the clock was quite a good enough reason for that deputy head to dismiss me, but there you go. What was his name? Mr Lee, I think; ah, the wonders of an eidetic memory.

Still, it's unlikely that what befell me might ever happen to a youngster passing through the education system today; thanks to the likes of Anna Kennedy, alongside the general penchant for increased awareness and tolerance – sometimes – there are now many more options for the young neurodiverse to explore, even in the aforementioned educational sense. There is a whole neurodiverse community out there now and what is still regarded in some circles as a disability has nevertheless become an identity every bit as valid as the various – and numerous – gender identities now available.

That isn't to say that there isn't still gross intolerance, however. I get particularly crazy whenever I think of the case of Andrew Young, the autistic man who was killed with a single punch because he remonstrated with a man riding a bicycle on the pavement. The killer, Lewis Gill, was sentenced to a mere four and a half years for the attack, and I remember the revulsion I felt when his mother spoke out in the press, saying that she couldn't see what all the big fuss was about. Anyway, I digress. The point is, perhaps this autobiography counts for very little and might simply serve as a parable about how bad things were for autistic people 'back in the day'. However, I'd also like to think that it – and particularly my educational achievements – might be seen as a slice of worthwhile narrative when it comes to assembling a chronology of the neurodiverse community, striving as they are to be regarded as something a little more worthwhile than just a bunch of side-lined, socially-awkward statistics.

It turned out that I had one final bit of educational reclamation to perform before I could consider myself fully recompensed. Before I could properly pass my PhD, I had to sit for what is known in academic circles as a 'Viva', which is an abbreviated form of the Latin 'Viva voce'. It's basically an oral exam, whereby you have to defend your thesis in front of a panel of esteemed academics, one of whom is an external examiner from another university; this person will often try and pick your thesis apart and do their best to catch you out. Apparently most people dread their Viva, but for me the angst was amplified because it was a face-to-face, several hours-long discussion of my work, and in most tutorials thus far I was having trouble enough knowing whether to look Shaminder or Jenny in the eye, as they batted about various ideas regarding thesis structure and the like. I exchanged emails with the university's disability officer but there wasn't much they could do by way of making allowances for my autism; I told them that if I could write the Viva I'd probably sail through it, but no, I would have to sit there and explain my thesis to this panel just like everyone else and there was simply no getting out of it. I had a 'mock Viva' with Shaminder and Jenny in the former's office by way of preparation, and at one point during the proceedings I got so stressed I almost had a meltdown. I was listening to Jenny but looking at Shaminder when it should have been the other way around, because Jenny was playing the crucial role of external examiner; when I noticed my mistake I threw my hands up in the air and I said to them, 'I can't do this!'; 'Yes you can,' Jenny said firmly. And so I tried again, only I was still focusing on Shaminder instead of Jenny; 'No, look at her,' the former snapped, 'don't look at me; imagine I'm the host, merely there to oversee proceedings, and that Jenny is the external examiner…'

'Yes, yes,' I said, 'but she isn't really the external examiner; you'll be there during the Viva, so why don't you pretend to be the external examiner instead.'

'Because that would be making it too easy for you, Mickey!'

A week later I had the actual Viva itself. I was surprisingly calm on the day, but it was the sort of resignation I guess people muster when they find themselves with no way out but to face the inevitable. I had half an hour with Shaminder beforehand to go over my notes one final time; she supplied the coloured stickers that might come in useful if I had to refer speedily to a particular page. As said, Shaminder would also be sitting in on the Viva but she wouldn't be allowed to intervene, merely there in her capacity as my tutor and to take notes on how wonderful/crappy I was doing. After that last brief run-through, we left her office and made our way around to the Keyworth Centre, a relatively new building which hadn't been part of the campus when I'd first arrived there in the autumn of 1998. The external and internal examiner and the host/chair were still busy with their ample buffet lunch and so Shaminder and I were relegated to a side room for fifteen minutes, to wait for them to finish; needless to say, this didn't do much to help my nerves. Eventually we were shown into a rather spacious classroom, with a fairly panoramic view of the rapidly regenerating Elephant & Castle just outside the window, overlooking the train station and the shopping centre in particular. Shaminder sat to my left – just out of view – whilst on my right was the external examiner, Dr Gareth Stanton from Goldsmiths. There was once a comic shop in New Cross, just opposite Goldsmiths, called 'Skinny Melinks', but I didn't bother with that by way of an icebreaker; I was too busy being intimidated by his casual academic confidence, in his flowery Hawaiian shirt, dodging the faintly dubious looks he was giving me over the tops of his spectacles. Of course, everyone present knew that I was autistic and that certain allowances were to be made, including what to do if I suddenly zoned out in the middle of a really important methodological explanation or something. The host/chair was a serious man called Dr Kenneth D'Silva, who regarded me curiously on a number of occasions but basically said little, as he was there simply to oversee the proceedings. I barely cracked a smile out of him even when the conversation somehow got onto 'Doctor Who', and how aghast I'd been – albeit temporarily – when I'd discovered that the 13th Doctor was going to be a woman, namely Jodie Whittaker. 'And so you see, Mickey,' he said to me, 'this is because you have been brainwashed by patriarchy.'

'But she'll never be as good as Tom Baker,' I protested.

'This is patriarchy talking, Mickey.'

'No, it's experience of Tom Baker talking,' I told him.

Of course I'd hyped the Viva up in my mind to the point where it became an impending disaster of almost epic proportions, but in the end I became so enamoured of my own proficiency in the subject at hand – subcultures centred around Anne Boleyn – that apparently no one could shut me up. Many laymen will be familiar with this particular portrayal of the average autistic person, i.e. the socially awkward geek who can't cobble a sentence together unless it happens to be based around whatever random subject they're obsessed with at the time. Well it just so happened that on this occasion my particular obsession was going to get me a doctorate and finally put to rest any ideas that I was either stupid or retarded; most people might have settled for an MA or two, but autistics really do tend to be rather 'all or nothing' sorts. Shortly beyond this point Jenny popped her head around the door – during the break – and by all accounts she said I was '…beaming from ear to ear'; maybe that was the moment when I was busy telling Dr D'Silva that, having seen the small teaser clip, I was nevertheless very much excited to see how Jodie Whittaker would play the role of The Doctor.

Eventually, the Viva finished and Shaminder, Jenny and I were ushered off to that side room to await the deliberations of the panel. The result would be either a straightforward pass, a pass with minor amendments, a pass with major amendments, or else the dreaded 'MFail'/MPhil. Jenny had brought a bottle of bubbly along with her, a sight that certainly buoyed my confidence as we sat there and awaited the panel's decision. Although I was fairly sure I wouldn't fail, I wasn't entirely convinced that I'd been so rigorous in my research that a year's worth of rewrites wasn't about to announce itself with the arrival at the door of Dr D'Silva. However, when he actually returned from overseeing the deliberations he said, 'We have some very good news,' and so it turned out that I'd passed, with minor amendments to address over the next three months. Jenny prompted popped open the bubbly and we all returned to the other room to toast my success, I for one very sincere and heartfelt in the way that human beings often are in the successful aftermath of high drama. Shaminder and Jenny were also congratulated for having successfully groomed another student, and I passed around my Little Book of Mary Queen of Scots in the hope that it might add to the lustre of having just achieved my doctorate.

After a while, I retreated into a corner of the room and then I thought to myself, Well I've reached practically the pinnacle of higher education, so what the f*** do I do now?!? – but I think then that Shaminder caught my mood; 'I'll tell you what you'll do next,' she said, after I'd given my doubts a good airing, 'you'll go out there and somehow you'll show everyone what a wonderful example you've set.'

In the lift, on the way back down to earth, Jenny then asked me how I was going to celebrate. I told her I was meeting Steve later and that we would probably go out for a meal; we did, to the Wildwood restaurant on Shaftesbury Avenue, opposite the latest incarnation of my beloved Forbidden Planet shop. But first I had to visit Neil's flat and change the cat litter for his two moggies; he was often away on business, so the care of the cats sometimes fell upon myself. And so, while most people would have been swigging more champagne, I was heading off to Sutton to shovel some cat shit. Make of that what you will.

Printed in Great Britain
by Amazon